Jessie Sale Lloyd

The Hazelhurst Mystery

Vol. II

Jessie Sale Lloyd

The Hazelhurst Mystery
Vol. II

ISBN/EAN: 9783337051556

Printed in Europe, USA, Canada, Australia, Japan

Cover: Foto ©ninafisch / pixelio.de

More available books at **www.hansebooks.com**

THE
HAZELHURST MYSTERY.

A Novel.

BY

JESSIE SALE LLOYD.

IN TWO VOLUMES.

VOL. II.

LONDON:
TINSLEY BROTHERS, 8, CATHERINE STREET, STRAND.
1877.

[Right of Translation reserved by the Author.]

CONTENTS

OF

THE SECOND VOLUME.

CHAP.		PAGE
I.	MARRIED AGAIN	1
II.	TWO GHOSTS	19
III.	MISS ANSELL'S LETTER	40
IV.	GEORGE SEES A GHOST	58
V.	THE GREAT MYSTERY	85
VI.	FATE	119
VII.	HARRY CARTLAND'S CONFESSION	130
VIII.	MISS ANSELL DOES HER DUTY	163
IX.	HOPES AND FEARS	168
X.	BERYL'S CHOICE	187
XI.	GONE!	196
XII.	DEAD!	201
XIII.	CONCLUSION	224

THE HAZELHURST MYSTERY.

CHAPTER I.

MARRIED AGAIN.

GEORGE GRAFTON, after some time answered the sad letters he had received announcing the death of his wife, but to Dr. Cartland he entered on his feelings as he did not to the others, telling him that he trusted to him to do in his absence whatever might be needful, as he should probably never again return to England, where he would be so forcibly reminded of his lost happiness.

Kate had been dead a year and a-half,

and Beryl had reached her eighteenth birthday. Of late the childishness of her nature had left her, she was now at seventeen years of age, a quiet and gentle woman, a mignonne little creature, very sweet to look upon. Her rippling fair hair, with the sun shining upon it, seemed like a halo around her innocent face, while the blue eyes would give out flashes of love-light when they rested on George, and the coral lips would smile happily. No one looking on would fail to read her secret, yet George Grafton was ignorant of it, thinking of her still as the child whom it was his duty to protect—of whom he had grown as fond as if she had been his own daughter, or younger sister, nothing more. Other love he had none to give, it was buried with his dead wife. So he never saw the light in Beryl's eyes that silently, though eloquently, spoke of love for him. Every one knew that Beryl Chantler was in love with George Grafton, except George Grafton himself. But people did not give him credit for this want of knowledge, and began to make unkind remarks upon the intimacy. If Grafton kept that girl in his household, they said, he ought to make her his wife. She was too young and too beautiful to live under the roof of a man of his age.

So poor innocent George was blamed undeservedly, without the least knowledge that he was supposed to be acting wrongly by Beryl.

He had planned for his overseer and his wife to live in his house and arrange it; this he supposed would satisfy Mrs. Grundy, and he had thought no more about it, having no idea what a disagreeable mischief-maker that good lady could prove.

These remarks began rolling about like distant thunder, when George's year of mourning was over; then people supposed he would announce his engagement, but as time went on and he said nothing, the thunder grew decidedly louder, and the lightning more forked, and now the storm was at its height!

The clergyman had made up his mind to "have an explanation with Mr. Grafton," and asked him to dinner for this end.

His name was Summers, and Charles Summers was his eldest and dearly loved son, who had left Ceylon shortly after taking George and Beryl there; had been back with his ship several times, on each occasion getting more and more enamoured with the fairy-like Beryl, but keeping the secret of his love closely locked up in his own heart.

It was only when he again returned and

heard all that was said of George and his idol, that he really knew how deep that love was, and he went straight to his father and confessed the whole truth, and Mr. Summers determined to "have it out with George."

The day of the dinner arrived, but with Mrs. and Miss Summers at the table nothing was said, and George was terribly "taken aback," when the three gentlemen being left alone, Mr. Summers suddenly turned to him and said, "When is your marriage to take place, Grafton?"

George turned white to the lips.

"I do not understand you, sir! I thought you knew that I have lost a wife I dearly loved, and that I could never replace her."

"I am sorry to hear this, Grafton; very sorry. I had hoped that your intentions towards that young and friendless girl were honourable, at least."

"What friendless girl?" cried George. "You cannot mean my little Beryl, she is a child, Mr. Summers!"

"She is, I suppose, seventeen or eighteen, and at any rate she is woman enough to love *you!*"

"Poor child," said George, "she is very fond of me. I knew her parents, you know, your son I daresay has told you how she came to me, and I hope I have done my duty by her, and made her as happy as I can. She has been a great comfort to me in my trouble, Mr. Summers, I assure you."

"If you don't mean to marry her, you are doing her a great wrong in keeping her under your roof, make all the amends you can. I will receive her until you can make arrangements for sending her to your friends."

George pondered.

"Do you really mean that any remarks have been made upon Beryl Chantler living in my house. Why, Mr. Summers, you must know, must have seen a hundred times, that I have a housekeeper—a woman of staid age —the wife of my overseer—the thing is absurd!"

"Absurd or no, you must show people that they have made a mistake, and you must send Miss Chantler to England."

"Poor Beryl," said George, "she will feel going among strangers very much. I wish she would marry; but if this foolish story gets about it would injure her, I fear."

Charles Summers flushed over face and brow, and then spoke earnestly.

"Grafton, I love Miss Chantler. I know she is as innocent as she is beautiful. I will shield her from any remarks, and will most proudly make her my wife if you think she will take me. I, like others, believed her love yours, and that you were only waiting to marry her until your time of mourning had expired; if I have wronged you, forgive me and be my friend with Beryl."

George Grafton took the young sailor's hand.

"My time of mourning will never expire till I do, Summers. I always fancied you cared for Beryl. I sincerely wish you success, my dear boy. I believe you are a good fellow, Summers, and that if Beryl consents, you will make her happy."

"Thank you, thank you, Grafton, I would lay down my life for her," and the young sailor seemed quite overcome by his emotion.

"When may I go to her?" he asked.

"Whenever you like—*now* if you please, or lunch with me to-morrow."

Mr. Summers here interrupted them.

"Not to-night, Charles—sleep upon it. Consider well if it will be advisable for you to propose to Miss Chantler. I own, under the circumstances, I consider it an unfortunate infatuation. Still, if it be for your happiness, I will not refuse to receive her as a daughter, for like yourself I believe her to be an innocent girl; but it would be indecorous for you to go to the house, knowing Mr. Grafton to be absent."

When the gentlemen parted, after a great deal of talk, Charles whispered to George to "speak a good word for him" tomorrow morning, and George promised.

After breakfast next morning, instead of going off to his work as usual, George lingered in the room. He found it very difficult to tell Beryl what he had to say, but at last he broke the ice.

"Beryl," he said, "come and sit by me," and she took up her old place at his feet, looking with her sweet smile confidingly up in his face.

"My little Beryl," he said, his hand wandering amidst her waving tresses, "it has been a great comfort to me to have you with me, but I am going to break up my home here and travel, and we must part, Beryl. You have been a daughter to the lonely man, dear child, and have helped me to bear my sorrow; but we must part now, Beryl! You have gained the love of an honest man, dear, and I hope to leave you the happy wife of Charles Summers. He is devoted to you, small Beryl—a second Samson and Delilah—and I hope you will try and return his love. It would make me happier to think of you in such safe hands, dear child. Beryl! try to make him happy, but if you cannot give him a wife's love I must send you to England to my mother. She is a good soul, and you will find her and my sisters kind, but I would rather you had a home of your own."

Beryl had listened with uncertain colour, and when he stopped she raised her eyes to his—such earnest, reproachful eyes, and withal so determined.

"I will not leave you," she answered.

"But, Beryl, child, you *must*. I am going to travel."

"I will go with you, Mr. Grafton."

A look of pain passed over his face.

"Child! child! how am I to deal with you?"

"I am not a child now, Mr. Grafton. Say whatever you wish to me; I shall understand you."

"Well, I believe it will be best to tell

you the truth, Beryl. People are cruel enough to misjudge me for keeping you here with me. After that, I should do you a grievous wrong to let you stay."

Beryl Chantler turned deadly pale, but showed by no other sign that she understood his words.

"Do you understand me, child?" he asked, with a shade of impatience in his voice.

"Yes," she answered, "I understand."

"And now, Beryl," he said, in a tone of relief, "you see why you cannot stay with me."

"I see, Mr. Grafton, that you are alone in the world, and that for my sake you would give up your home. I see," she added, with rising colour, "that I have no one in this dreary world but you, my friend and protector, and though I feel the cruelty of the remarks made upon such kindness as yours, I will not leave you."

"Beryl, child! if you wish to please me, you will accept my friend, Charles Summers; he is worthy of your love. Please me by marrying him, dear."

"Mr. Grafton, I cannot."

"Beryl! naughty Beryl! What am I to do with you? Will you go home to my mother?"

"George," she cried, and large tears gathered in her eyes, "don't send me away! I love you. I love only you in all the wide, wide world. Never send me from you. I cannot go. I don't ask much," she pleaded. "I know, oh! how well I know, your heart is with her; but let me be your little Beryl still, as I have been now for so long. I can comfort you, George. I can make your life less lonesome to you, that is all I ask, let me be with you; never send me away." And Beryl hid her tearful face, half-ashamed at her own boldness.

George Grafton was troubled—more troubled than words could express. He rose and left the room, and with hasty and uneven strides walked up and down, down and up, his garden.

"What can a man do, with a woman who is such a child! and yet the child is a true woman! Beryl, Beryl, what can I do with you?"

Charles Summers at last arrived, and asked eagerly whether George had said anything to Beryl.

"Yes!" said he, "I have told her my wishes on the subject, but she is such a strange child, I cannot make her out. Summers," he exclaimed, after a pause, "try your best with her! it is a matter of the utmost import to me that she should marry. I have tried to explain to her what the world thinks of her position in my house; but she is too innocent to understand it. There seems but a choice of *two* things; if you don't marry her, I must, and God knows, how bitter it would be to me, to be unfaithful to the wife of my love! I have walked up and down here for three hours, and have fought a hard battle with myself, and have come to this decision."

Charles Summers looked at him, then grasped his hand.

"You're a good fellow, Grafton. I see you wish me well with her, but sooner than her good name should be affected, you will sacrifice yourself for her sake. However it ends, God bless you! Now, shall I go to her?"

"Yes, and God prosper your suit, for all our sakes."

The luncheon-bell rang, and George went in. He met Charles Summers at the door.

"I can't stop to-day, Grafton! She wont have me at any price; wont give me one ray of hope. George Grafton, she loves *you* with all her heart and soul. You will make her your wife?"

"Yes, I will," said George; "and I will try never to let her know what it has cost me."

"We shall not meet again, Grafton," continued Charles Summers. "So long as I know you are in the island, I shall not return here. I shall hear about you all from my father. Good-by."

The men shook hands again with a hearty grasp, and parted; each with a heavy heart.

When the shades of evening were closing in, George Grafton took Beryl by the hand, and led her out into the garden.

"Beryl, dear! why did you refuse to be Charles Summers' wife?"

No answer.

"If I had asked you instead, would you have refused me?"

Beryl burst into tears.

"Answer me, little one; do you love me enough to have said, Yes, if I, had asked you to be my wife?"

"I never knew you unkind before, Mr. Grafton," she said, between her sobs. "What pleasure can it be to you, to make me confess what I should do under impossible circumstances?"

"But, suppose they are not impossible circumstances? Beryl, will you be my wife?"

"You say it out of pity," she cried.

"I say it, Beryl, because I wish it; because only as my wife I can keep you with me. Will you leave me, child, or will you be my wife?"

"I will be your wife, George," she answered, trembling painfully at the unexpected joy. "I will never leave you."

So George Grafton took Beryl Chantler to be his wedded wife, and vowed to love and to cherish her till death should them part.

CHAPTER II.

TWO GHOSTS.

GEORGE and Beryl did not leave Ceylon, but lived on, in the same house they had occupied for the last two years. Beryl had had one year of unalloyed happiness. Are there many who can say as much? A whole year of satisfied love, and perfect contentment; so who should say that Beryl had not done well with her life. Little loving Beryl clung to her husband as the ivy to the oak. The oak might have had no wish to wear the ivy, but he gives it his strength nevertheless, and never shows a sign of dissatisfaction; and the ivy twines round him lovingly, and keeps him green amidst the wintry blasts, until he knows he would feel bare and cold without his feeble dependent.

The ties that George had taken upon him out of a sense of duty had now become very dear to him. He could never love his little wife with the ecstatic devotion he had given to his stately, beautiful Kate. *She* had been a queen among women, and had commanded his worship and devotion; but he grew very tender towards the fragile little creature who nestled in his breast and called him "husband" with such loving pride. They were very happy, these two—never dreaming of the days of blackness to come.

"What trouble could reach her as George's wife, with him to take care of her?" thought trustful Beryl, basking in the warmth of his love and kindness; and yet there was a cloud in the horizon, no bigger than a man's hand as yet, and still unseen by them. The cloud was in this wise.

Miss Ansell's lease was up, and her landlord intending to live in the house himself, would not renew it, but he had a neat, old-fashioned cottage near Maidenhead, and if his tenant liked, she should have it at a moderate rent. Miss Ansell went and saw it, liked it, and concluded the bargain, little dreaming that the hand of Fate was leading her into a land of horror, madness, and death; that her sense of duty would be put to the test for the exposure of sinners, and the breaking of the hearts of the good. Had she known it all, probably she would not have hesitated; she knew but one creed, and that was duty. Duty was her God—God her duty. The cry of the Publican was foolishness to her; she had no patience with those who did wrong, and then went cringing for forgiveness. She thanked God—like the Pharisee—did her duty, and needed no repentance. Dear, good, strong iceberg that she was. No! ice will melt, but not so Miss Ansell. The simile is bad. She was of the hardest flint—of iron, of steel, a petrifaction—and yet she really always did what she conceived to be her duty, and, judged by the letter of the law, and weighed in the balance, she could not be found wanting, but she knew not "charity," and surely every other Christian virtue combined, fails to make harmony without that sweet key-note; and Miss Ansell's life was out of tune, discordant, grating. In the old dispensation, when men took an eye for an eye, a tooth for a tooth, she would have been a fine specimen of humanity, but, judged by the light shed upon us by the undying love of a dying Saviour, Miss Ansell's religion was unlovely, not pure metal.

She took possession of her cottage, and in due time had settled down into her old groove. She was a great walker, holding the doctrine that God would not have given people legs and feet if He had not intended them to be made use of, and old though she was she certainly made good use of hers. She went into Maidenhead twice a week to do her marketing; and on one of these occasions she saw—*Two Ghosts!*

A face from the dead, and a face of death. She was just about to cross the road, but waited for a carriage to pass. It was going at a rapid pace, drawn by two fast-stepping bays. It was a close carriage, and both the windows were up. It passed her as a flash of light, and yet she stood transfixed—rooted to the spot—for once in her life frightened out of her calm coldness, for she had seen *two ghosts*.

She laid hold of the arm of a policeman who was passing.

"Whose carriage was that?" she cried.

"Carriage?" said No. 101, coolly, "I don't see no carriage, mum."

"There! there!" shrieked Miss Ansell. "There! going away in that cloud of dust! Quick—quick? I shall lose the clue!"

The policeman eyed her keenly. Mad, or drunk? was the problem he was trying to solve, and he paid but little attention to the receding vehicle, but her bony fingers clutched him with such a vigorous tenacity as to arouse his temper.

"Come, ma'am, you'd better move on, or else I shall be under the painful necessity of taking you in charge for obstructing the thoroughfare, for assaulting me, and otherwise breaking the peace. Come—move on, I say" (as Miss Ansell showed no inclination to let him go).

"Then you wont give me the information I require?" she asked, resuming her usual manner.

"I'm not paid to answer impertinent questions. What does it matter to you whose carriage it was? You didn't think as any one was running away with yours," he said ironically, " now did you? because in that case, it would be my duty to help you, you know."

Miss Ansell was shrewd; and looking at the avaricious face before her, she said—

" I'll give you half-a-crown for your information."

" Oh! that alters the case," said he, smiling, " but in my profession the fees are paid in advance."

Miss Ansell took a well-worn leather purse from her pocket. It was never very full, and after the unusual expenses of moving, it was now particularly empty, but she selected, one shilling, a bent sixpence, two threepenny and one fourpenny bit, one English and one French penny, thereby making up the promised half-crown, and counted them into the policeman's ready palm, meanwhile taking a mental note of the number on his collar!

The man grinned at the motley little collection of coins, and transferred them to his pocket. He had not the remotest idea whose carriage had passed, but he knew that a Mr. Andrews, living close to Maidenhead, owned a similar vehicle to the one he had seen in the distance, so he made up his mind that it was the same, caring very little whether he was right or wrong, and he said, unhesitatingly—

"The carriage belongs to Mr. Andrews, a retired City gent; lives at Fair Lawn, about half a mile out."

"Are you *quite* sure?" Miss Ansell asked.

"Quite;" and they parted, each to go their own way—No. 101 to his favourite "public," on the strength of so much small change, and Miss Ansell straight to Fair Lawn.

She went boldly to the hall door and knocked, asked if any one was at home, and was at once admitted and ushered into a gaudily-furnished room. On the table stood an enormous candelabra of solid silver, filled with gorgeous artificial flowers, magnificent cabinets stood around the room, on the top of which were groups of alabaster and Parian marble figures, chiefly *un*draped; the walls were one mass of looking-glass, the corners of the room were cut off with inlet glass, making it octagonal in shape. There were panels of looking-glass all round the room; what amount of wall was left visible was painted—wreaths of flowers on a white ground. The curtains and furniture coverings were of richest yellow (almost orange) satin damask; in fact, everything bespoke heaps of money and lack of taste.

No one was in the room, and Miss Ansell had ample time to take in her surroundings, which she could only compare with horror to her own holland-clad little chamber, and shudder at. A fit place to find her, indeed! The house must belong to a Turk, and this must be his divan. Mr. Andrews! and yet that other face—altered, but still his. Well!

whoever the place belonged to, it was self-evident that it was a den of iniquity. "What Christian would live in such rooms?"

And then the door opened, and a large, handsome, vulgar-looking woman entered, and eyed Miss Ansell curiously. This woman looked kind and good-tempered; but all that the old maid saw was that she was over-dressed, and was "powdered," and in her mind her character was simply gone.

The large lady bowed, and waived Miss Ansell to a chair, but that virtuous creature would not bow to this "painted Jezebel," as she had called her in her mind, nor would she sit down in such a house. The Venuses and Cupids round the room made her wish to hide her maiden head or their nakedness. She longed to be back in her own decent parlour, where even the legs of her pianoforte were clothed; but here these nude figures stood boldly round on all sides, reflected everywhere by the everlasting mirrors. Whichever way she looked she could see them. She would have rushed from the room, but duty kept her there.

The large lady sat down and began feeling for her purse. This nameless visitor must want a subscription, probably was the representative of some missionary society, or wished her signature to a petition for "woman's rights."

"You have come on behalf of some Society, I suppose?" she said, with a good-humoured smile. "Well, I shall be happy to subscribe. I consider the rich ought to help the poor. It is not in my line to go into dirty, stuffy cottages myself; but I am always ready to assist those who like that sort of thing. Now don't be afraid to tell me what you want, I have plenty of money," and she rattled her well-filled purse.

Miss Ansell took no notice whatever of what she should have seen at once was good-natured vulgarity, nothing worse.

"Who are you?" she demanded, sternly.

Mrs. Andrews laughed till she shook.

"I really think I ought to be offended at being asked such a question, but I suppose you don't mean to be rude, my good woman."

"Is this Mr. Andrews' house?" asked Miss Ansell.

"Yes. it is. We have purchased the freehold. Beautiful place, isn't it?"

"And you are——" interrupted the old maid.

"I am Mrs. Andrews!" answered that lady, with conscious dignity.

"And you have a dark green carriage, drawn by two bay horses?"

"We have."

"And it has been out this morning—passed through Maidenhead about an hour ago?"

"Good gracious me!" cried Mrs. Andrews, "what can you know about me or my carriage, you strange creature? I must say I think you are cool, and to say the least of it, not polite."

"In that carriage," continued Miss Ansell, ignoring her remark, "was a young woman of two or three and twenty, with a pale face and dark hair; also a dark man with a black moustache, dark eyes, and a face paler than I have ever seen before. It was not always so pale."

Mrs. Andrews was now watching her anxiously.

"I see you recognise them," said the old maid.

"What of them?" asked Mrs. Andrews, nervously. "They have gone for a drive, and are not home yet, and the horses are fresh ones, surely you have not come to bring me bad news! surely nothing has happened!"

"I have come to do my duty. Ay, even i she were my own child I would do it all the same. I have come to denounce her and the villain who was by her side, and having done that I will write to her husband, and now I wish you, good morning."

And before Mrs. Andrews could recover her presence of mind Miss Ansell was upon her road back to Maidenhead, and Mrs. Andrews had come to the alarming conviction that she had enacted the above scene with a mad woman, which was, no doubt, about the only one she was likely to arrive at.

She was still sitting in a most perturbed state of mind, when a young girl of about two-and-twenty entered the room, followed by a dark young man some three years older. These were the son and daughter of Mr. Andrews and his buxom wife.

"Oh, my dear children," exclaimed that lady, "I am so relieved to see you back, have you met with any accident or annoyance?"

"None whatever, mamma," answered the girl. "We have had a delightful drive; we have been to Cookham to call on the Laws'."

"Did you see a strange gaunt-looking woman—straight up and down like a yard of pump water, in Maidenhead?"

"My dear mamma, I have just told you we have been to Cookham, we have not been near the town, and we have not seen any old woman at all!"

"Who is the person you refer to?" asked young Andrews, with languid interest.

He was one of those listless creatures who had "seen life" all through at twenty-five, and was now longing for a new sensation. Everything that money could buy him he had, but he was unable to purchase "an object in life," so he had to exist without one, and found that existence was but a dull business, notwithstanding his gold, carefully amassed and scraped together by that "City gent," whom policeman No. 101 had referred to—a good hard-working vulgarian whom this elegant son called "governor," and looked upon solely as the "paymaster-general," and was heartily ashamed of, for being unrefined and innocent of the letter H.

Mrs. Andrews fanned herself with her handkerchief.

"Oh! my dear boy, I wish you had been

here to protect me! I have been alone with a mad woman!"

"Well, my dear mother, all I can say is, you don't look any the worse for it. What was the sensation, pleasant or otherwise?"

"Don't laugh, Randolph. I assure you, however I may look, my nerves are dreadfully shaken. Oh! she was such an alarming creature, I couldn't help thinking of Solomon Eagle in 'Old St. Paul's,' when she threw out her arm like an avenging spirit, and denounced you and your sister."

"Denounced us!" cried the young people together. "Why! what for? What have *we* done?"

"That was what I wanted to know, but she rushed off like a whirlwind! Oh! my dears! I am sure I have had a wonderful escape, we ought all to be very thankful.

She couldn't be Solomon Eagle's sister, but she might be his niece. Dear me! let's see, how many years ago was the fire of London, when Solomon Eagle denounced the people from the roof of St. Paul's?"

"Never mind about the Fire of London. mother, tell me about this old mad woman, I am quite curious about her," said Mr. Randolph Andrews.

"There's not much to tell," said his mother.

"Simmons (the butler) informed me that an elderly party who didn't give her name was waiting for me in the drawing-room, and I went down, and saw a very tall old woman standing in the room, badly dressed; she might have been a broomstick dressed up for a scarecrow, with a wooden face, for all the expression or figure she had. Well, you know, *we* have no shabby genteel acquaintances on our visiting list, so I supposed she was come begging for some charity, and I took out my purse at once ready to help her."

"Just like you, mamma," said Alice, "always ready and willing to do a kind action!"

Mrs. Andrews answered her daughter's compliment by a resounding kiss, most heartily given and smilingly received.

"And to go on with my story, children. She didn't want money, and I don't know even now what she did want! She described the carriage and horses and both of you to the life, and then denounced you solemnly!"

"How strange," said Alice.

"It seems to me, mother, that the only moral to be gathered from the story is this: *Never admit elderly females, or any one else, who does not give his or her name ;* and I will go and give Simmons orders to that effect," said Randolph Andrews as he sauntered from the room.

CHAPTER III.

MISS ANSELL'S LETTER.

THE outraged spinster rushed home, satisfied that she had at last found out the mystery which had enshrouded the death of George Grafton's wife. She had but little knowledge of vice, but believed the world to be full of it. Often and often she had brooded over the events of three years ago, until the most simple facts became distorted to her mind, and now she had come accidentally upon the sliding panel, which it was her duty to push back boldly, and expose the crime in all its blackness to the world. She knew of George Grafton's second marriage, and condemned him for it. Marriage at all, under the most favourable circumstances, she disapproved of; but for a man or woman to marry twice, was a fault not to be overlooked. She thought George Grafton a reprobate, and worthy of no consideration at her hands. So she wrote the bare naked truth, as she believed it to be; her letter ran thus :—

"DEAR SIR,—You will possibly remember (unless your mind is too much occupied with the cares of a second wife), that when my niece died suddenly, I considered the circumstances surrounding her death peculiar and suspicious, and that I had them investigated fully. I did my duty, and had to rest satisfied that I had laboured under a mistake; but often since then my mind has misgiven me, and I have feared that after all there lay some deep hidden mystery in the affair; and now I write to inform you that my forebodings were correct. I have left my old neighbourhood, and am now residing near Maidenhead-on-Thames. While in the town to-day, I saw your wife driving *with* Dr. Cartland! they did not see me, and I need not say that I have no wish to renew their acquaintance. I considered it, however, to be my duty to trace them, and I called a policeman who informed me that it was Mr. Andrews' carriage, and that he lived at Fair Lawn. I had no difficulty in finding the place, and went in unannounced; that is, I gave no name. The inside of the house stamped it as the abode of iniquity. A painted Jezebel received me; she called herself Mrs. Andrews, no doubt your wife does the same. I suppose it is one of those dreadful Mormonite establishments which that horrible Dr. Cartland keeps here, regardless of the laws of the land; but what can you expect from an unbeliever? George Grafton!

I have done *my* duty, it is now for you to do *yours*. I have found your wicked wife, it is for you to expose and punish her. I did not see her, as the painted woman said she was out, but I described her and the man, and saw by her face that I had made no mistake.

"Yours truly,

MARIA ANSELL."

When George Grafton received this letter his indignation knew no bounds. This hard, wicked old woman had seen some one like his darling Kate (his darling still, though dead—though replaced by another —yet she was his heart's one and only love still, and must ever so remain), had chosen to imagine it was her, and Heaven only knew what steps the interfering old wretch might take, bringing scandal upon the woman in her grave.

"I must go to England at once, and prove to the old idiot that she has made a mistake—a cruel, dastardly mistake—my poor girl! my beloved wife, that such a slander should be named in the same breath with you. Kate, Kate, I am faithful to you still, although I needs must cherish the little creature washed up by the sea for me to take care of. My poor little Beryl, she will not like to part from me, and yet she cannot come now; but the baby will keep her from fretting after me. May God bless my boy, my first-born, and his mother, little sunbeam that she has been in my dark days. I grieve to leave them both, but my first duty is to Kate."

He left the room and the house, and went straight to the doctor's.

Dr. Mills looked up, startled at the pale, stern face before him.

George had not for a moment believed in the accusation against his dead wife; but that letter seemed to have raised the devil in him. He was impatient to be off, to disprove the foul lie against his dead love.

"Nothing the matter at home, I hope, Grafton?"

"Nothing in the way you mean, Mills; but there is a great deal the matter with me. To doctors and lawyers one may tell one's secrets without fear of being betrayed, May one not?"

"To some," answered Dr. Mills, with a smile; "but don't put too much trust in either."

"You, at any rate, are a good fellow, Mills, and I can, and *will* trust you. You know Cartland, do you not?"

"Of course, I do."

"Then tell me what you think of him?"

"Oh!" said Dr. Mills, "my dear fellow, if you want an opinion you must go to the other trustworthy profession, and for six and eightpence you will get just the reverse opinion to what you want, whatever it may be!"

Even in Ceylon people had heard of Mrs. Grafton's mysterious death, and that Dr. Cartland's name had been unpleasantly mixed up with it. So Dr. Mills was not very anxious to express his real opinion of the man, to that woman's husband, as it was by no means flattering to the noble doctor.

George Grafton placed the letter he had just received in the hands of the medical man.

"Read that Mills, and tell me what I ought to do."

The other read it through attentively—

he did not tell George his thoughts, for he believed in Miss Ansell's vision, had always considered Mrs. Grafton's death a most extraordinary affair, and now he was far from anxious to enter upon the subject with George. He put the letter back into the envelope, and laid his hand on George's shoulder affectionately.

"It is a painful letter for you to receive Grafton, but my advice to you is to try and think no more about it, and not even to answer the letter of this disagreeable meddler in your affairs."

"But, my dear Mills, I must go and clear my wife's name from this slander. I must prove her innocence."

"Innocence is its own advocate, Grafton. You have another wife to consider now, as sweet a wife as God ever blessed a man with, and a son; your duty is to take care of them, not to run the world over disproving statements (which no one will believe) of a crazy old woman. Surely Grafton you are too sensible to go off on such a wild-goose chase! You must remember these are not the days of trap doors, sliding panels, and mysterious disappearances."

"I never thought they were," said George, smiling in spite of himself. "You don't think I believe these lies against the truest woman God ever made, nor have I any reason to believe Harry Cartland to be anything but a man of honour. We were college friends, and he was a wild lad; but since we have renewed our acquaintance I have found him a staid, quiet man."

"Under these circumstances, my dear Grafton, have the sense to remain by your wife's side, that is your right place now," said Dr. Mills.

And George left him, silent, but unconvinced. After wandering aimlessly about, he suddenly turned his steps homewards, and went to his wife's room. What a picture met his eye. A fair head, with waving, rippling hair, falling on a snowy pillow, a pale sweet face bending over a rosy one week old babe, which was nestling in her caressing arms, safely clutched by two tiny fragile little hands, which peeped out from the ruffled sleeves of her wrapper, and then the face was raised to his, brimming over with wifely, motherly love.

"Come, George, and help me to find out the colour of baby's eyes; are they like yours or mine? Oh! I do hope they will be like yours, George."

He stooped and kissed the mother and child.

"I wish I were an artist, my little Beryl, I should just paint you as the Madonna and Child. You can't tell how lovely a picture you two are together."

"Oh, George! I *am* so proud, so happy," cried out this child—wife—mother—and then, with love's intuition, she looked at him more closely, and the joy faded out of her face.

"Husband!" she said, in a pleading tone, reaching out her little hand, "something is the matter, tell me what it is."

"Nothing, dearest."

"George, I know better; do you think your words can deceive me, when I know every expression of your face by heart? Something has troubled you deeply, dear; you think to spare me, but, believe me, I shall suffer more if you keep me in the dark. Trust me, husband, you will find I can be very brave."

George sat down by the bedside, and rested his aching head upon his wife's pillow, in silence; and after a while began. "You have guessed rightly, Beryl, darling, I *am* in trouble, and I will explain it to you so far as I am able to do so. You will not mind my talking of Kate, little one? You know I love you, dear, but you also know how devotedly I loved my first wife?"

"Yes, yes, I know!" murmured Beryl, with a trembling lip. "It is quite natural George, I do not mind."

The spirit of the small creature was brave; but the eyes, bright with unshed tears, rather belied the words.

"If any one slandered you, my Beryl, what do you think I ought to do? What do you think I should do?"

"You would defend your wife, I know, George," answered she with a happy smile.

"Yes, dear, and punish the person who had wronged you."

"No, George, not if they were sorry for it; we would both forgive them, dear, knowing that we ourselves need so much forgiveness."

"My precious, gentle little wife, you are right, darling, not if they were sorry—we would, as you say, forgive them if they repented of their sin."

"But, George dear, what has any one said against me?"

"Against you, my child? The slander has been against my Kate—against my first wife."

And a shadow of pain crossed his brow. Beryl sat upright and looked at him.

"No, George, no, there must be some

mistake, the worst person living would not slander the dead!"

She looked now unlike the gentle girl who wished to forgive her enemies; it seemed to her true nature that to malign those who had no power to defend their good names, but had gone to answer before a higher tribunal than that of man, was a sacrilege—an impossible, unforgivable sin.

A sad smile was all his answer.

"What!" she cried, "some one has really spoken evil lately of your — of Kate?"

She could not call her his wife, even now.

"Yes, dear Beryl, some one has invented the most horrible, cruel, dastardly lies against her. Now, tell me what I ought to do. I ought not to sit still and hear it, little one, ought I, when she cannot defend herself?"

Beryl turned very pale, but put her hand into his.

"I cannot advise you, George, for you are far wiser than I am; but do not consider *me* if you think you have any duty to perform to her."

"God bless you, my wife," cried George Grafton, catching her to his breast. "You are a noble, brave little woman, Beryl. I love you, I am proud of you; what other woman would have been so unselfish? I do think I have a duty to perform, I will go to England and clear that poor girl's name, and I will soon be back with my blessed little wife here. Oh, child!" he cried passionately, "if any evil were to befall you through me it would break my heart, my pure dove," and he smoothed the fair disordered tresses of silky hair, as they lay negligently on the pillow, nestling about her slender throat.

"What evil can befall your wife, George?" she asked, with a happy, contented smile.

"God grant, none, my dearest, but I am full of forebodings of evil," he answered gloomily; and then, as if determined to shake it off, he smiled, and said, "you ought to be flattered, little one! that the prospect of leaving you for a few short weeks should take the pluck out of me like this; and I am very wrong to worry you thus; I hope you wont miss me very much, dear," he added lovingly, "you will have my son to take care of you in my absence."

"God bless our child!" said the mother, drawing him more closely to her, and stooping to kiss his infant lips.

"Amen!" answered George to her petition.

After awhile, she said, " When shall you go, husband ?"

" I don't know, Beryl, but by the very first steamer."

" Because," she continued, " I should like baby to be christened before you do."

" Very well! wife of mine, you shall have your wish. I will go up at once and ask Mr. Summers to baptize the boy before I start;" and he rose to go.

" George," said Beryl, " you have not told me what has been said against her, against Kate, you know."

He was going towards the door, but stopped suddenly and looked at her, all the colour gone from his face. With her words there flashed upon his mind the consequences that such an accusation proved would have upon her, his present wife; if that were true, not his wife at all, and then he cast the thought out of his mind as if it had been a poisonous reptile.

"No, Beryl," he answered, "I cannot tell you what it is; it is not fit for your pure ears to listen to, your pure heart to ponder over. Beryl!" he cried, with subdued passion, "I would sooner die than that you should know and realise such a story as I have been told about poor Kate," and he turned and left the room without another word.

CHAPTER IV.

GEORGE SEES A GHOST.

BABY GEORGE was made a Christian of, and a tender parting had taken place between George Grafton and his wife. She kept up a brave spirit till the last; till the last sound of the wheels had died in the distance, which were carrying from her what she loved best in the world; and then she gave way to her grief. She never thought him unkind to leave her, never tried to persuade him not to go; he had told her it was his duty, and Beryl was the last little woman in the world to wish to stand in the way of that. She said no more about the nature of the slander against the first Mrs. Grafton; but she very often wondered about it, framing what she thought dreadful things, that some one might have invented; though never in her innocence coming near to the black truth. But George's earnestness, George's words were for ever presenting themselves before her. "He would sooner die than that she should realise such a story." Poor George! How tender he was over her, and her wifely heart sang anthems of praise for the gift of such a husband as George Grafton!

So days and weeks passed on, and George had reached England, and had seen Miss Ansell. From her house he walked straight to Fair Lawn, sent in his card, and was admitted to the sanctuary of mirrors, golden damask, and statuettes. He could not help smiling as he cast his eyes around the gorgeous room, remembering the anathemas he had just heard hurled upon it by Miss Ansell's Christian lips; upon it, and the house, and all that dwelt therein. He could understand that Miss Ansell would be horrified, though to him, the undraped Venuses being only works of art, he could look at them with pleasure, each being perfect of its kind.

While he was gazing at a reclining Venus in a looking-glass stand, the door opened, and George turned round, a cry escaped his lips! "Kate!" he cried, in an agonised voice, and sunk into a chair, and covered his face with his hands.

The girl looked very much alarmed, and made her escape from the room.

"Another mad person!" she exclaimed, as she rushed into her mother's boudoir. "Oh, mamma! I will never go and receive strange visitors for you again!"

"Why, good gracious me! what has happened, child?" asked Mrs. Andrews, struggling into a rich green silk dress.

"Mother?" cried Alice, "there's a madman in the drawing-room."

"Lor! there must be an asylum let loose! Oh, dear! I wish your pa was at home, or Randolph."

"Be quick, mamma, for the man's ill as well as mad! I was afraid to stay by myself; but I'll go back with you."

"And we will tell Simmons to wait outside the door," said the mother.

In the meantime, the deadly faintness that had seized upon George, as he saw a tall, dark, graceful girl, dressed in white "piqué," with a bunch of crimson roses at her breast, enter the room, passed away; and he looked up to find that he was alone.

"Good God!" he groaned; "was it a delusion of my excited fancy? did my brain call up a picture of my dead wife, as I used to see her, that happy summer-time, three years ago? Has no one been into the room after all?" He wiped the drops of agony from his brow, his hands were cold as clay. If that were Kate! what, what, was she now, and Beryl, and the child, what of them? "Oh, God!" he cried, "deliver me from this ghastly fancy, it cannot be real!"

Again the door opened, and a lady appeared, who in a moment he recognised as Miss Ansell's "painted Jezebel;" yet she was *not* painted. Nature had blessed Mrs. Andrews with an all-powerful colour; which that good lady had endeavoured to soften down with an unlimited supply of violet powder! George felt relieved, as he looked at her; he saw at once, that vanity and vulgarity, were the greatest sins that the stout lady had to answer for. Alice, walking in her mother's shadow, was at first invisible through Mrs. Andrew's bulk. He started, as she once more appeared. They had now come close to him.

"Mr. George Grafton," said Mrs. Andrews, looking at his card, " I don't think I have had the pleasure of hearing the name before."

George had never taken his eyes off Alice's face.

Mrs. Andrews made a gesture of introduction. " My daughter, Miss Alice Andrews," she said, grandly, with a majestic sweep of the arm.

An expression of inexpressible relief passed across his face. George Grafton was himself again! Not only had Mrs. Andrews' words lifted a weight from his heart, but on close examination he found the likeness to his dead wife in this girl before him, though great, was not nearly so great as his excited imagination had supposed. Her face was not as perfect in features as Kate's had been; still they were alike enough to have been sisters—quite.

"Mrs. Andrews," said George, "I must ask your pardon for my peculiar behaviour to your daughter, but her extraordinary likeness to a dear wife whom I lost three years ago, must be my plea for your forgiveness."

There could not be a kinder-hearted woman than Mrs. Andrews; and an honest tear twinkled in her eye as she stretched out her hand to George, thereby offering him her friendship.

"Oh! Mr. Grafton, don't worry your head about that! you frightened Alice a little, but she'll get over it. I am sorry you have had your troubles; so young too, and so gentlemanly-looking. I've quite taken a fancy to you, Mr. Grafton, and I hope we shall be friends, but I can't help laughing, for Alice took you for a lunatic!" and the worthy woman gave way to an uncontrollable fit of laughter and shaking; "and only to think," she continued, "we've got Simmons outside the door, now (that's the butler, you know), to protect us if you proved dangerous!" and Mrs. Andrews laughed again, shaking like an animated rouge mange!

Alice coloured.

"You must excuse my thinking so, you know, as you were peculiar; and we had a fright from a mad woman, about a couple of months ago."

"Yes," said George, "she wrote to me,

and told me that my wife's death was an imposture, and that I should find her here. My dear Kate died while I was in Ceylon, just a year after our marriage. You may imagine, Miss Andrews, when you came into the room, looking so like her, dressed in her favourite costume of white, and crimson roses, how you startled me!"

"I am so sorry," said Alice, sympathetically.

"Why, it's quite a romance!" said Mrs. Andrews, smoothing down the green silk with a caressing hand. "And now you've come to England to look for another wife, I suppose, Mr. Grafton?" she asked, while her eyes rested on her daughter's handsome face.

"No! on the contrary, I have married again, which made the idea of my first wife being alive a doubly serious matter to me."

"Only to think of that!" cried Mrs. Andrews. "You thought you had committed bigamy! No wonder you were frightened at our Alice, when you thought she was your first wife come back to accuse you of your falseness!"

"No, Mrs. Andrews; no thoughts of myself were in my mind when I saw your daughter. If you knew how I loved Kate, you would understand it better."

"Kate," said Mrs. Andrews, "was that number one, or number two?"

"Kate was my first wife's name; my present wife is called Beryl."

"Present wife," laughed the stout lady; "that sounds as if you were going to have half-a-dozen more!"

George looked serious, and Alice was quick to perceive it.

"Beryl!" she said, "I never 'heard that

name before, how pretty it is. I feel sure any one owning it must be very charming."

"My little Beryl is an angel, Miss Andrews. I should like you to know each other very much; you are so like the one I loved best on earth, that I know you must be all that is good, and I wish I could insure your friendship for my wife, who is quite a child."

"You are right there, Mr. Grafton," said the proud mother. "Alice is as good a girl as ever stepped in shoe-leather; not one of your district-visiting sort, who pretends to be in love with every dirty child she sees, and to enjoy the smell of poverty, that you find in squalid cottages, and the chance of bringing home more than you took out! Alice is too refined for that sort of goodness; but she doesn't spare her pocket-money, if she knows a poor person is in want; and she works at her needle for them like a lady, and makes them clothes."

Alice looked up. "I wanted to have a district, but mamma would not hear of it; and she gave me such a graphic description of all I should have to go through, that she quite horrified me. The poor must live in a dreadful state."

George looked at her kindly.

"And how are they to learn better, Miss Andrews, if no one will teach them?"

"Then you approve of ladies taking districts?"

"Certainly, I do. It is the sick who need a physician, not the healthy; the ignorant who require teaching, not the learned."

"Come, come, Mr. Grafton, please not to put such ideas in Alice's head. I have only one daughter, and I don't want to see her die of scarlet fever, or small-pox, which she's sure to take, having had neither. No, no, Alice; give away as much money as you like, but give it with the tongs, as one may say. If you hadn't got money to give, I'd say nothing; but your money does them more good than your words, I'll warrant ; and if you want to teach religion I'll send for as many bibles as you like, and one of the gardeners shall go round with them. Not one of the indoor servants, for fear they should bring home anything. The fear of infection, and insects, is the terror of my life, Mr. Grafton," she ended, pathetically.

George and Alice both smiled. How like Kate she was. It gave him quite a painful pleasure to be near her.

" Mrs. Andrews, I am trespassing too much on your time, I fear."

"Not a bit of it, go home and dress yourself, and share our dinner. Randolph is going to bring a stranger home this evening; some one he knew when he was at Oxford. Randolph is my son, you know; and then you will meet Mr. Andrews, too. He's not much to look at, is he Alice? But he's a good hand at making a fortune; and he's an honest man. Randolph looks down on his father; but for all that he's been a good father to him, and never denied him anything in his life; but then, you know, Randolph has been at the University, and is rather a swell!"

George had been going to refuse the invitation, but he feared lest he should be supposed to look down on the absent Mr. Andrews, so he said, kindly—

"I shall be very pleased to make your husband's acquaintance, Mrs. Andrews.

Every honest man has a charm for me, and I feel sure I shall like Mr. Andrews," and he held out his hand to say good-by.

"Well, *au 'revor,'*" said she; "we dine at seven to the moment, no grace allowed, Mr. Grafton!"

"I will be punctual," laughed George, as his eyes rested once again on Alice's face.

George returned to Miss Ansell, and told her of her mistake. A great weight had been lifted off his mind, his spirits were elated, he felt as if he walked on air. There was nothing against his darling Kate, nothing to come between him and Beryl, nothing to break her faithful heart, and take away his son's very name. And George was thankful, very thankful, and very happy. He would go back to his little wife, and small son, as quickly as possible, only running down first to see his father and mother. He sat down and wrote to Beryl a joyous letter—the last she ever had from him—full of love and brightness, over which she laughed and cried, by turns; inexpressibly happy that the shadow had passed out of his life, that she should see him again so soon. He was coming back, he said, as fast as steam could carry him!

And Beryl was happy, telling her joy in broken words to the babe upon her knee, who threw up his small arms at his mother's voice, as if he understood her words.

George Grafton spent a pleasant evening with the Andrews. Randolph condescendingly patronised him, the old man gave him a hearty, H-less, welcome. Alice liked and admired him, and Mrs. Andrews patted him affectionately on the back!

The stranger collegian was a slight

acquaintance of his own; had joined the University about the time he had left, not even at the same college; still they were acquaintances, and both had known Harry Cartland in those old days.

"By-the-by, Grafton, do you remember a man at Oxford, named Cartland?"

"Yes," said George, "he and I were at the same college."

"Poor devil!" continued he. "He has come very suddenly to the end of his tether. Cartland has had a short life and a merry one!"

George Grafton looked very grave.

"Poor Cartland! dead, is he?"

"Well, not actually dead; at least, I have not seen it in the *Times*, but he is given over."

"Poor Cartland! We were friends, and his approaching death is a shock to me."

"Wild dog," continued the other. "Some story about his murdering some other man's wife about three years ago."

The evening was over for George. So there had been such talk as that about his wife—well, it was time to say good-bye, and he said it, amidst a running accompaniment of regrets from his hosts and hostesses.

A dull sense of pain went with him to his hotel, and continued all night, mocking the elasticity which had defied trouble all the day through, since his interview at Fair Lawn with Mrs. Andrews and her daughter. He felt angry with Dr. Cartland, then angry with himself for his want of feeling for the dying man. How could he help the scandals got up by the world against Kate; or, indeed, were they not against the man himself? He would go to London and call upon him, and shake his hand once more in this world. Having made up his mind he was anxious to be off at once, and rose early for his start. London reached, he hailed a Hansom cab, and drove straight to Dr. Cartland's door. The hall-porter was a stranger to George Grafton.

"Dr. Cartland had been out of town for these two months and more. He could not give his address—believed he was living near Windsor. All letters were addressed to the Windsor Post-office, to be called for. The practice was sold to Dr. Duval, who was at home then. Would the gentleman see him instead?" "Yes—George Grafton would. No—he would not send in his card."

"Dr. Duval would see the gentleman at once. The practice had fallen off in Dr. Cartland's hands after the *talk* about Mrs. Grafton; the ladies became afraid of him, and he was less sought after. Dr. Duval was *not* a favourite with any one. He looked like a foreigner, but spoke good English. No one seemed to know anything of him until he came into Dr. Cartland's business."

George was shown in; the two men bowed. George was the first to speak.

"You are Dr. Cartland's successor, I believe?"

"Yes; what can I have the pleasure of doing for you?"

"I shall be much obliged if you will give me Cartland's address," said George.

Dr. Duval eyed him keenly.

"You forget, sir, that you are a stranger to me."

"True," answered George, "but I am a friend of Cartland's. We were at college together, and now I hear that he is ill."

"Very ill—in fact, dying," said Duval.

"Do you attend him?"

"I do."

"Then undoubtedly you can give me his address."

"Undoubtedly I could," said he, coolly; "but Cartland is a friend of mine, and I see no reason for telling his whereabouts to every one who may ask for it."

"But why not?" said George, greatly astonished.

The doctor shrugged his shoulders.

"Does a dying man want visitors?"

"Then you wont tell me where he lives?"

"Exactly so!" answered Dr. Duval, with an amused smile.

George thought for a few moments, and then took out his card and handed it to the other.

"You must have heard of me if Cartland

is a friend of yours. As a stranger, you will not assist me I see, but as a mutual acquaintance of the same man you can hardly withhold such a small civility."

Dr. Duval looked at the card, and even his mask-like face underwent a change, and George noticed it.

"I see you have heard of me," he said.

Dr. Duval seemed uncertain what course to steer, and then, after a pause, answered—

"Yes—I see no reason for denying that I have met with the name before. I was called in to see a lady of the name of Grafton about three years since who was dying, and it seemed to me a sad case, for she was all alone—no one with her but her medical attendant."

George's lips trembled. Here then was another witness to poor Kate's death.

"I am that lady's husband," he answered.

"Good God!" exclaimed the doctor, surprised out of himself. "I thought you had died abroad, been lost at sea, or something of that sort; I am sure I heard so."

"Did Cartland tell you so?" asked George, sternly.

"I am not prepared to say, one hears a great many things without being able to remember who was the originator of a report. People will say anything, Mr. Grafton. I actually heard some say they had seen your wife within the last twelvemonth, yet I saw her die!"

George turned clay cold.

"Who said it?" he asked, with suppressed passion. "If it be a man I will break every bone in his body!"

Dr. Duval smiled, and again shrugged his shoulders.

"My dear sir, you have lived some time

abroad; you must have forgotten the ways of the world. It is impossible to trace these little 'on dits.'"

"Then I will make you responsible for them," said George, sternly. "No one shall say or repeat anything against my dead wife if I can help it."

Dr. Duval looked at his watch.

"I am always sorry to part with pleasant society, Mr. Grafton, but a medical man's time is not at his own disposal. I must wish you good morning," and before George could stop him he had passed through a mysterious door which was papered over, and had not been noticed by George before, and was gone.

George Grafton tried the handle, but the door had evidently shut with a noiseless spring, and before he could gather up his scattered senses, a servant entered the room to show him out, and he had nothing to do but to go. On and on he walked, and entered St. James's Park, and at last stopped by the ornamental waters and sat down.

The walks were utterly deserted—the shuttered windows of the London houses seemed to bespeak a dead world. If any human beings were alive in those mansions, they must have lived in the back rooms, for the sake of appearance; for who would be in London in September?

A dreadful weight was on George Grafton's heart and spirits. He seemed lost in the shadow of a dark and unknown evil. For hours he sat looking into the still waters, with a terrible longing to find rest in them from the nameless horror that was upon him, a longing which he put from him impatiently.

" My mind must be upset," he said aloud,

not noticing a policeman who was standing behind him listening to his words. "What do I imagine? what are my fears? I cannot tell; and yet I seem driven on to some unknown misery. Why cannot I be content to go back to my wife and child, and find happiness, instead of prowling about England in search of a mystery which probably does not exist? I wish I had followed Mills's advice, and never come over on this wild-goose chase. Just when I thought I was free to go home, this Dr. Duval arouses fresh doubts in my mind, and yet, what did he say to do so? He declined to give me Cartland's address. Why should he do so? that is what I have to find out next."

The policeman scented business, and walked round him so as to get a good view of his face.

"Windsor Post Office!" cried George, starting from his seat. "That is where I must go," and he made off across the park.

The policeman watched the retreating form, muttering to himself that he expected he should see that gent again; and straightway pulled out a little note-book and entered the words he had heard George speak on a blank page, which he headed " A Mystery," and very much satisfied with his own acuteness he "moved on" to look for other interesting matters.

CHAPTER V.

THE GREAT MYSTERY.

DR. CARTLAND was very fast approaching the Valley of the Shadow of Death, but his dying hours were cheered by a loving woman's devotion. She was seldom away from his bedside. Night and day she smoothed his pillow, raising the emaciated form in her strong white arms, and resting the weary head upon her breast. The sick man's eyes would rest upon her full of gratitude and love, and he would kiss the hand that ministered to his wants.

"My darling," he said, "I shall soon know the Great Mystery!"

Large dark circles surrounded the beautiful eyes of the girl he addressed, and spoke of nights of weary watching; and the agonised expression of those orbs told a tale of suffering enough to melt a heart of stone.

"Oh, Harry!" she cried, burying her face in his bed-clothes; "oh, Harry! do not leave me. I have no one—no one but you. Let us call in fresh advice; surely among all the clever men in London *some one* could be found to cure you. Oh! why —*why* must I lose you?"

He lifted his feeble hand with difficulty, and stroked her glossy dark head.

"No one can cure me, my darling; my hours are numbered."

The girl sobbed piteously.

"Why, darling, it is not often you give way," he continued. "Be brave still for my sake. Oh, love, when I think of all you are to me, all you have done for me, I find it very hard to die, little one. In the days to come, if you ever feel inclined to blame the dead man, remember that you were his one and only love!"

She nestled closely to him, but answered by no word. He seemed exhausted from the effect of talking, but soon renewed the conversation.

"In after-life, love, if you find I have deceived you, could you forgive me?"

"Forgive you, Harry—what could I not forgive?" cried the heart-broken girl. "You know I would give my life for you, my love—oh! my love!"

"I shall die happier for that promise, wife," he said, with a faint smile. "I have kept but one secret from you. You will know it when I am gone. I have written to you, and you will open the letter after I am buried—not before."

Choking sobs alone told him that she heard him.

"I have not behaved well to you, love, but you have promised to forgive me. But, darling," he said, almost raising himself in his earnestness, "never doubt *one* thing, that my love for you was the one true and pure feeling of my life; that I die loving you in death, as I have loved you in life; and if I were not an unbeliever, I should hope to renew that love hereafter. Dear love, can there be any meeting again for us? you who are a true Christian—I an unbeliever. The one honest feeling of my life has been my love for you, and that a good man would count unholy, a thing to be repented of, and I cannot repent of it. Oh, my darling, my more than wife! I glory in it. If I believed in God, I would thank Him for these three years of perfect happiness, and ask Him to give you back to me in another world; but as a man lives so must he die. It is too late to change now; I have lived an unbeliever, I must die an unbeliever," and he sunk down on his pillow exhausted.

"Harry," whispered the girl, gently, "we have both sinned, but the blood of Jesus Christ cleanseth from all sin. For His sake we shall be forgiven."

She rested her pale cheek upon his thin hand lovingly, and thus they remained silently for a long while, and then he looked at her sad and weary face.

"My darling, you are worn out; you will not distress me, love, but will go and rest for a couple of hours."

"Don't send me away, Harry," she pleaded.

"My wife, I must insist; I will have one of the servants to sit with me, but rest you must have, and now, or you will break down; kiss me, love, and go."

The girl rose wearily, and kissed him passionately, and then left the room with heavy, listless steps, and in a few moments more a man-servant entered.

Harry Cartland would have no woman save his wife in his room.

"What time is it, Stevens?" he inquired of the man.

"Three, sir!"

"Have the letters come?"

"I will see, sir," and presently he re-entered with several on a salver.

Dr. Cartland had written to London to his lawyer, and here was an answer from him, to say he would be with him at "three thirty," and then the sick man glanced through his other letters, and laid back on his pillow to rest.

"I shall want pens and ink ready, Stevens, and my desk. I am expecting a gentleman presently, you can leave when he comes; draw up the blinds, and let me look at the light of the day," he added, languidly.

For the last month he had been too weak to walk upstairs, so a room had been arranged for him upon the ground floor—a pretty room, draped with delicate crétonne, a room in which every detail showed a lady's hand; flowers from the lovely garden were arranged tastefully here and there, nothing was forgotten that the sick man liked. The French windows were opened upon a soft, green, well-kept lawn, roses peeped in round the window sills, while clematis hung festooned about the top. Willows bowed their weeping branches to the gentle breeze, kissing the water as it rippled past. The cottage in which Dr. Cartland was living, was called

"The Nook." It was close to the Thames, but lay back in a pretty little winding back-water, so that it could scarcely be seen at all by the passers-by on the river. It was hidden too by the luxuriant shrubs and trees by which it was surrounded, disclosing nothing but a few chimneys and gables to the world. It lay in from the main road also, having green fields stretching as far as eye could range, and gates up the carriage drive to the house—an isolated place although in the midst of habitations.

This was the home to which Harry Cartland brought the woman of his love—the wife of his heart, nearly three years since.

About noon this day (the day on which Harry Cartland was expecting his lawyer), a gentleman walked into the General Post Office at Windsor, and asked for Dr. Cartland's address; each official referred him to another, not knowing it, till he found himself before the postmaster, who was intensely civil, also intensely ignorant as to what he wanted to know.

The inquirer was George Grafton. He repeated again his question, patiently, having asked it some half-dozen times before.

"Could the postmaster give him Dr. Cartland's address?"

"No!" the postmaster "regretted very much he could not oblige him. Dr. Cartland lived a long distance from any post office—somewhere up the river—and always sent to Windsor twice a-week at least for his letters. Mrs. Cartland had been for them herself more than once, and a sweet looking lady she was; would make a most lovely widow! for the poor doctor was on his death-bed, and indeed to-day was the day for fetching the letters; if the gentleman wished to send any message, he would take care it was delivered to the groom, who always, at least generally, rode over."

"No, George would not send a message, he would look out for the man," and Fate helped him, for as he turned to leave the office, he felt a mysterious tap on his shoulder, and there stood the postmaster by his side.

"There! that's Dr. Cartland's groom, sir, dismounting at the White Hart," he whispered confidentially.

"Always glad to oblige, sir," said the man, in answer to George's thanks.

George Grafton crossed to the hotel yard, where the man had led in the horse.

So Harry Cartland was married, and he had never heard of it, and now his wife would be a pretty widow!

Poor Cartland! and that was all the world said or thought about the affair.

He walked up to the groom, and asked whether Dr. Cartland was any better.

The man shook his head.

"No, sir, nor never will be in this world; he's took to his bed now, poor fellow, and he'll never get up no more, and missus is just heart-broken."

"I am very sorry, indeed," answered George; "how long has your master been married?"

"Don't know, sir, at all. I have only been with him a year, and I never thought to ask; but they seems to be all in all to each other, as the saying is."

"Ah!" said George Grafton. "Well, I am going over to see Dr. Cartland this afternoon, and am not sure of the address; be good enough to give it to me!"

The request, being accompanied by half-a-crown, was acceded to at once, and the groom having got the letters, rode off again at a brisk trot for "The Nook," and mentioned faithfully to his master's man, his meeting with the gentleman at Windsor.

So when Stevens heard that Dr. Cartland was expecting his lawyer, he put two and two together, deciding that they were one and the same person.

The bell rang, and Stevens went out of the bed-chamber to usher in the stranger, and as he closed the door he was puzzled by hearing his master exclaim—

"Grafton! Grafton! is it really you? you in the flesh?"

George walked up to the bedside, and took his wasted hand in his.

"Don't," cried the sick man, shrinking back; "I have injured you."

George looked at his hollow cheeks, and saw he was in no state to be agitated.

"Say you forgive me, George, and I shall die happy! What brought you here? I thought you were out there in Ceylon, married and happy."

"I heard some rumours of Kate's not being really dead, Cartland, and I came to England at once."

The sick man's face grew ghastly as he listened; death seemed to be coming upon him; he clutched the bedclothes between his clammy hands convulsively.

"I have seen Dr. Duval," continued George, "and he tells me he was with her when she died, so it is impossible for me to doubt any longer. So you are married, Cartland! Good God! what is the matter?" for the sick man had fainted.

George rang the bell, and the faithful Stevens entered the room.

He looked reproachfully at George.

"You might have seen he was in no state to talk to or be agitated," he said roughly; "but some folks have no feelings for others; poor master?" and he set to work at once to try and bring his master back to consciousness.

He chafed the thin hands, held salts to his nostrils, and wetted his lips with brandy.

Blood oozed from his mouth.

"Had you not better fetch Mrs. Cartland?" said George.

"I think not, sir," said the man; "and if you will take my advice you will go before he comes to."

Just at this juncture the lawyer, whom Dr. Cartland had expected, entered the the room, and the gentlemen mutually inclined their heads, neither knowing who the other was.

The dying man once more opened his eyes, and looked with a scared gesture around him.

"You here still, George!" he groaned. "You told me you forgave me, Why, why, don't you go?"

"What was it Kate said? 'The blood of Jesus Christ cleanseth from all sin!'"

"Amen," said George Grafton,

"Were those *her* last words?"

Harry Cartland's head had been wandering, he now looked at George as if he did not fully comprehend.

"The last words she spoke before she died, poor girl, I mean," explained George.

Dr. Cartland groaned.

"Grafton, I have written you a long letter. In that I have told you all there is to tell with reference to Kate. I have not the strength to talk to you now—in pity leave me. You will not have long to wait," he added, with a sickly smile; "give your address to my good lawyer here, and the day I am buried he will deliver my letter to you in person, and help you like a true friend in the difficulties I have brought upon you."

The lawyer here whispered to George his advice to leave the room, and George Grafton's and Harry Cartland's hands clasped for the last time, the men parted in silence, and when George Grafton quitted the room Stevens went with him, and Dr. Cartland and his lawyer were left alone. He pointed to his desk.

"In there you will find my will," he gasped, "all my papers of importance, and some letters, which are to be delivered the day of my burial. When you have looked over them all you will find that there has been a mystery in my life, and I want you to know that Mrs. Cartland was not a party to the deception I practised. Remember this, as the last words of a dying man, and be a friend to her, Saunders."

"I will," answered the man of law; "I promise to befriend your wife."

Dr. Cartland turned to him with a gesture as if on the point of making a disclosure, and then sank back.

"Not while I live," he murmured. "You will all know the worst soon enough, it wont be long."

The door opened softly, as a pale girl entered with gentle footsteps.

"Shall I be in the way?" she asked, with a sad smile.

"Is that you, darling?" said Dr. Cartland, the light of love illuminating his dying eyes, "I hoped you were sleeping, dear love."

"I could not sleep, husband, I dozed once, and woke with such a horrible dream, and even after I was awake voices from the dead sounded in my ears. Oh, Harry, I heard George's voice so plainly. Oh! what have I done?" she cried. "Husband! husband! speak to me, and you, Mr. Saunders, will you ring for Stevens."

She had seen Mr. Saunders before—he had come down to witness Dr. Cartland's will with his clerk; but he had said the will was not to be read by any one, not even by his lawyer, while he lived, and after being duly signed, it was sealed up, and he kept it in his own desk. Mr. Saunders had been touched by Mrs. Cartland's tender devotion to her husband, as well as attracted to her by her beauty, and most willingly he undertook to be her friend. A pleasant, and not difficult task, he thought, to be the friend of a rich and lovely young widow, especially, being a bachelor himself, with very little interest in life, and only a moderate amount of clients, and therefore only a small income. He was a man with an honest and good heart, which accounted perhaps for his not having got on better, for Sydney Saunders was not fond of dirty work, and would never take the case of a "black lot" in hand. His friends told him he would never get on, he was "too conscientious." His enemies called him a "prig" and a "fool," but Sydney Saunders still continued his usual road, making enough to live on, and none to spare. His thoughts had wandered from his work to

Mrs. Cartland and her husband's approaching death. He pictured her in her beauty and loneliness, and sighed to think how little it was in his power to do for her in her sadness, and as was his custom when in thought, he fell to humming to himself—"What will to-morrow bring? Who can tell?" when his office door opened and admitted George Grafton.

The gentlemen had exchanged addresses the day before in Harry Cartland's bedchamber.

Mr. Saunders was rather surprised to see his visitor, but received him courteously. George could hardly explain what he had come for, he knew that the letter which was to tell him something, which he had to forgive, would not be delivered till his old friend was at rest in his last earthly resting-place. Impatience for that time would simply be indecent on his part, and yet he was impatient, not impatient for the death of the man who had been his friend, but to know what the mystery was that hung over his life and enshrouded the death of the wife he had loved. Through the slowly dragging hours of the night he had, bit by bit, formed theories, only to cast them aside again; but the last one that had taken possession of his mind seemed possible, and became fixed there.

Perhaps Cartland was aware that he had not called in medical help in time, he might even know he had mismanaged the case, and that poor Kate had been a victim to his want of care, anything worse than this must have been found out at the postmortem. As for Kate being alive that was simply impossible. Cartland himself had certified to her death, and Dr. Duval had been in the room when she died, and all at Hazelhurst House had identified her. There was no room for doubt about any of those facts. But having arrived at this satisfactory conclusion, poor George Grafton found sleep none the more easy to woo, and he tossed restlessly till daylight, and then having refreshed himself with a cold bath, descended into the unswept hotel among the sleepy unwashed waiters who were just beginning their day by clearing up, and by noon found himself sitting in Sydney Saunders' office. That worthy man looked at him scrutinisingly.

"You are out of sorts, Mr. Grafton. A hard night, I should say," he added, with a smile.

"A very restless one," said George, "for I never closed my eyes once, and was floundering and gasping for breath all the time, in the middle of a huge feather bed. The man who invented feather beds ought to be introduced to the rack, or the thumbscrew, for the tortures he has brought on the mass of humanity who have suffered from his invention."

The two men looked at each other, and each acknowledged to himself that the other was an honest man, if appearance went for anything, and as if mutually drawn together, they shook hands, and then Mr. Saunders invited George to be seated, and they fell into talk, during which Sydney had mentioned Dr. Cartland's beautiful wife, and her devotion to her husband—had acknowledged not to have known either of them more than a year and a half—had settled a few little matters of land for Cartland, and had gone down about his will, and had remained there a day or two as guest to the young couple, with whom he was charmed.

"And you don't think there is any mystery about his marriage?"

"None whatever," he answered energetically; and then there flashed across his mind Dr. Cartland's words that there *had* been a mystery in his life; but it could not refer to his marriage, for he had solemnly assured him that Mrs. Cartland had *not* been a party to it; but he turned the subject as quickly as possible, feeling that he was treading on dangerous ground, and asked George to dinner, and he accepted the invitation.

"Bachelors' fare, you know, Grafton, and lodging-house cooking," he said, with a laugh, "so bring a good appetite with you."

When we last saw into Harry Cartland's

sick-room, he had fainted at the words his wife had uttered. But she, and the attentive Stevens, soon brought him round again; and Mr. Saunders took his leave, accompanied by the desk which the dying man had placed in his charge.

Then husband and wife were left alone. For the most part, they were silent; the silence only broken, now and then, by words of love on either side.

Harry Cartland was sinking fast. All night she watched him in the dimly-lighted room; watched him with dumb agony, tenderly kissing the hands that lay almost passive in her own.

This then was the end of it; her life would cease with his. Not so far as animal existence went, but all that made life worth living for would be gone! nothing but the *husk* would be left to her.

Ah! how she wished that she could give up life with him, that she might be permitted to enter the dark valley by his side. She should not fear the blackest shadows, if she were facing them with *him*. But to remain behind, to meet the cold looks of the world alone; there was no one to whom she could apply for comfort.

By her own act and deed, she had shut herself out from all her former friends. Even her husband, who loved her more than life, felt this, and would never let her go anywhere, where there was the faintest possibility of recognition. She felt somehow that she was shut out from the world, but she counted the world well lost for love. And love she had, earnest, passionate love, strong even in death!

Early next morning, Dr. Duval arrived, and after speaking to the sick man, he signed to the poor wife to follow him from the room.

Dr. Duval's manners were generally rough, but as he took Mrs. Cartland's hand in his, and looked at the white face, drawn with care and sorrow, his voice almost shook, as he told her, she must "be prepared for the worst." He told her he would return directly he had seen his patients, he thought her husband might live yet a few hours, but he would not last through another night.

Mrs. Cartland knew it all before, yet it seemed to fall with an overwhelming, crushing weight upon her. She staggered, seeing which he took her arm, and led her to a chair.

"Try and bear up, for his sake," he said, in a low voice. "Death is a hard thing for a man to face, Mrs. Cartland; make it as easy to him as you can, don't let him suffer for you too."

Dr. Duval had struck the right chord. Mrs. Cartland looked up.

"You are right; thank you for what you have said, Dr. Duval. I will be brave for his sake; it will be time enough to think of my sorrows when his are over, poor darling."

"You are a noble woman, Mrs. Cartland. I wish there were more in the world like you!"

His words seemed a pain to her.

"My only merit is loving my husband, Dr. Duval; and it is lucky for the world there are not many who love so well. Women without hearts have the best times of it; they take the happiness out of their lives, grow fat, never weary themselves, and are perfectly contented. And yet," she cried, passionately, "I would not give up the glorious happiness of the last three years, for thirty of the ordinary lives of women!" and then she added, piteously, "don't think me rude, but don't detain me, our time is so short together now; don't keep me from him!"

"One word only, Mrs. Cartland, you will be very ill if you keep up this strain upon mind and body much longer; take an hour's rest."

"Not a moment," she cried, impatiently, making for the door. "What time will you be back?"

"As soon as possible; about three or four."

"Then, good-bye for the present."

The weary-eyed woman was soon beside her husband's bed again.

"I need not ask what he said to you, love?"

She was silent.

"I know I shall not live out the day. Keep quite close to me, love. I am too feeble to feel for you."

She nestled beside him on the bed.

"That's right, dear love, I shall now feel your sweet breath on my cheek, the warmth of your dear arms about me. Perhaps, I shall sleep a little, love; don't leave me, no, not for a second."

Sometimes he stirred, and when he did his wife seized the opportunity of giving him his medicine and champagne. He could no longer eat.

Dr. Duval came again, and offered to remain; but Dr. Cartland shook his head.

"I know what that means, but I would rather die in her arms alone."

"But, Cartland, you must think of her, would she not be afraid if you got worse?"

"My blessed wife will not be afraid of me, alive, or dead, Duval!"

And she held his death-cold hands, and answered him with a smile.

Dr. Duval shook the dying man's hand.

"So be it then, but I shall not leave the house, and if I am wanted, you will know I am on the spot. Good-by, Cartland. May God give you rest!" and he left the room.

The dying man refused all further nourishment.

"Don't offer me any more, love."

So the wife crept up again beside this one she had loved, who was now passing so quickly away from the reach of her love and tender care, and tried to keep him warm; but the death-chills would not be stopped by human hand.

His mind wandered over his past life, which he referred to in broken words. He talked with horror of a death, and of a funeral; but she did not know of whom he spoke; he was asking George Grafton for his pardon, and then he begged for hers, till her gentle words recalled him to himself, and he would lay quiet, and then he fell asleep, his head pillowed on her breast. His mind was tortured even in his dreams. At last he sprang up, as if he had regained his strength.

"Come away, Kate!" he cried, "quick, quick, they have discovered the mystery. Say, you will never leave me, Kate ! nothing shall part us ! Kate ! you are my wife; Kate !"

A stream of blood was rushing from his mouth, making his protest against their parting a ghastly mockery.

Mrs. Cartland put out her hand to reach the bell, but there was a look of reproach in her husband's eyes, which she understood. He had recovered from the terror of the dream, which he had been unable to shake off, at first, upon waking.

Mrs. Cartland understood that he wished still to be alone with her, and she did all in her power to stanch the blood, which flowed for some time; and then she took her place beside him once more. He was prostrate from exhaustion, but a smile lit up his face, as she laid her hands upon his feeble ones; and so he sunk quite gradually away, power of speech was lost in weakness, till just at the last, the flame of life gave one bright flicker, and he said—

"Remember, love, I love you to the last!"

Once more he opened his eyes.

"Those words, Kate; what—were those words? *the* blood?"

And Kate fell upon her knees, holding the almost dead hands, and breathed that blessed promise into the failing ears of the dying man, who had lived an unbeliever; and she saw that he believed at last; for a glorious smile of intelligence passed across his ashen-hued face—lending a beauty even to death itself—and all was still. The spirit had fled, but the smile rested still upon the lifeless clay.

And Dr. Harry Cartland was gone, as he said, to solve the Great Mystery, which, sooner or later, every man must do for himself.

CHAPTER VI.

FATE.

WHEN Mrs. Cartland knew that death had indeed overtaken her husband, a stupor fell upon her, and she remained for hours upon her knees by his side.

Dr. Duval had peeped into the room when darkness set in, and found that utter silence reigned.

He roused the prostrate woman, and led her forcibly from the room, and tried to get her to partake of food, but she turned from it with loathing.

He made her swallow a little wine, and she sat with wide open, haunted eyes and listless hands, gazing into space, endeavouring to see through the barrier which divided the finite from the infinite, which kept her from still seeing her love.

After awhile she rose and crept back to her dead; the moonlight shone upon his beloved form—how precious the cold clay, even, was to *her*.

So she passed the night kneeling there beside him, till morning dawned,

George Grafton went to dine with his new friend, Sydney Saunders, and the two men suited each other.

There is no better cement for forming a friendship than that fact. How often people, both estimable in their way, may be found who don't get on and never will, simply because they don't suit.

Troubled as he was, George felt a pleasure

in this man's companionship; and while he was with him he almost succeeded in putting dull care aside; but when at eleven o'clock he found himself alone again, walking back to his hotel with the September moon shining on his path, a new restlessness seized upon him.

He would go down by the night train to Windsor, and walk over to "The Nook," and inquire for his old friend. Of course he would not go in, for had they not taken their farewell of each other; there was no reason on earth for his going—it was a trick of fancy which led him on—it was inexorable fate!

George walked from the station, feeling no weariness in the fresh morning air. Came upon the river banks, and stopped to watch the circles made by rising fish, or angler, playing some monster jack on greedy feed, as jack nature is of early morns.

He took pleasure in the songs of birds above his head, or in bushes by his side; marked the fresh stacks of harvesting just thatched with golden straw; wondered at the early smoke that rose through the clear sky from the thrifty cottagers' breakfast fires, lighted thus soon to send the workmen out armed for their toil, and then he came within sight of the gables of "The Nook," and started to find himself there, as if he had come almost without his own consent or knowledge, and what was he to do since he was here?

It was too early to rouse even the servants in the house—only five o'clock—and still he wandered on, opening and shutting gates mechanically, as if he had a fixed purpose, but he had none.

He entered the shrubbery, and walked

into the garden looking at the flowers, and rested on a seat, from whence he noticed that all the blinds were down, except in one room downstairs, which was, he fancied, the room occupied by the dying man. This he thought so strange, that he longed to know why it should be so; blinds up and an open window, enough to kill any sick man outright.

George was not inquisitive by nature, but fate was too strong for him.

The soft lawn went straight up to the window; no crunch of crisp, pebbly gravel announced the footstep of the intruder, and on he walked to his doom.

Will nothing in heaven or earth stop him ere he looks into that room? Has God no pity, that he can permit a guiltless man to suffer as if he had been the vilest thing on earth?

Kate! here is Nemesis at last, after your three years of bliss! the relentless finger of fate itself points the way to the unveiling of the mystery.

How now for Beryl's broken heart?—innocent, lovely, loving Beryl! Yes, she too must suffer, and her unconscious, nameless child. The guilty one has passed to a higher tribunal and smiles still, at the blessed promise of forgiveness by Kate's side.

George Grafton went up to the window opened to the ground, saw the dead man lying on his bed with placid upturned face; saw a woman kneeling by his side as if in prayer, her dark head buried amidst the tumbled clothes where she had writhed in agony and misery, praying wordless prayers for resignation, and for the peace of the soul of her love.

What should George Grafton do there, intruding on the grief of the sorrowing wife of his dead friend? and yet something in the *pose* of the prostrate woman chained him to the spot.

Had his salvation depended on his walking from that sad sight without another look, perdition must have been his doom!

His whole being was concentrated into one sense; he watched as if his very life depended on what his sight could reveal to him! Yes: and how much more than life!

At last, unable to control himself, he stepped into the room, and the movement aroused the mourner.

She gazed at the intruder with wide-open, horror-stricken eyes—gazed speechless with agonised terror; while *he* stood equally horribly, silently transfixed.

Each to the other in belief—DEAD!

There, between the two men who had loved her, both of whom she had loved—but in so different a way—Kate stood, and if sin can be expiated by suffering here on earth, hers must have been blotted from the book of life. Great drops of agony rose like pearls upon her ivory brow.

After a silence which seemed a lifetime to each, George pronounced her name.

The well-known voice struck upon her ear, and was answered by a piercing shriek from the wretched woman.

"What!" she cried, "have you come back to life to reproach me? Why do you not rest in your grave! Oh! George, I was fond of you, but I loved him—oh! I loved him."

He advanced a step towards her, but she waved him back wildly.

"Back from the dead!" she shrieked—"back from the dead! you have come to divide us, but no one can do that—keep off! keep off! you shall not touch him!"

Her eyes flashed out lurid light, her white arm extended to keep evil from her dead.

Her shrieks and excited tones aroused the household, who flocked to the room pale and wondering.

Dr. Duval was the first to enter. Even he could not understand the scene, but he saw at once that Harry Cartland's widow was raving mad.

The day of the funeral arrived at last, and by force they had to remove the mad woman from the room, which she had never quitted since she had seen George Grafton, as she supposed, arisen from his grave, to part her from her lost love. And now, with the cunning of madness, she watched the sad procession depart.

Finding herself locked in, she clambered from the window and followed on foot, never losing sight of the hearse containing her dead.

They lowered the coffin into the grave.

"Dust to dust" had been solemnly pronounced by the officiating clergyman, when a terrible scene ensued.

Kate, unseen before, came suddenly into the midst of the astonished party, and raising her hands and eyes passionately to heaven, she cried, "My love! my love! I will never leave you," and fell with a wailing cry heavily to the ground.

Her grief and beauty touched all who were present, and she was gently raised and placed in one of the carriages, and conveyed back to "The Nook," and soon put under the care of a keeper, for she was pronounced a confirmed maniac, of whose recovery there was but little hope.

CHAPTER VII.

HARRY CARTLAND'S CONFESSION.

GEORGE GRAFTON was completely stunned by the discovery of the wife he had mourned as dead, being alive as the supposed wife of another, the agony of mind that he suffered being increased by the impossibility of extracting a word of explanation from the senseless maniac. The burthen of her cry being that he had come back from the grave to part her from her love. Her love! Ah! the agony to that faithful heart in those self-condemning words! And agony was heaped on agony, when he remembered that other wife of his, that patient, loving, little being who awaited his coming in a distant land, but to return to whom now, would be a sin, black as night.

In his despair the kind face of Sydney Saunders came before him, and he turned his back upon that house of death, madness, and sin—out again into the fields; not now seeing God's hand in the works of Nature around him, but going on—on, blindly, on.

At last he was standing at the office door, a wreck of the man who had left it but the day before; sunken cheeks and hollow eyes told their tale of suffering.

"Good God! Grafton, what is the matter with you?" asked the lawyer quickly, as he looked inquiringly at the other.

And George Grafton told the story right through to his new friend, from the time he had parted from his wife at Hazelhurst, up to the present, when he had left her a maniac at

"The Nook," clinging to her beloved dead. As the story proceeded, Sydney Saunders could scarcely restrain his excitement. He listened, holding his breath lest he should lose a word. And now the tale was begun and finished, and he found that the woman for whom he had taken a romantic fancy, had a husband living still, though one was deceased, and she was mad.

And then there returned to his mind the words that Dr. Cartland had used when he asked him to be his wife's friend.

"What do you make of it all?" asked George.

"Why this, Grafton, that Dr. Cartland has played a villain's part, and that however wrong your wife may have been in her love for the man, she is innocent of any connivance with, or knowledge of, this shameful plot."

George grasped the lawyer's hand.

"Thank you, for those words, Saunders; weak my wife must have been, but I can never believe in her guilt, poor Kate! poor Kate!" And then, after a pause, "And now I want your advice. As a man of honour, what can I do? You know I have married again, and I have a son by my second wife. Oh, God!" he groaned, "never my wife, but as pure as an angel of light. In pity tell me—tell me what I can do, how I can act in such a maze of iniquity. Whatever course I take, it seems to me, must be fraught with ruin to her—my loving Beryl. To return to her as her husband, would be blackest treachery and sin; to leave her alone, to bear the shame I have brought on her and the child, would be cruelty."

"Perhaps some honest fellow will make her his wife, and comfort her with his love,

Grafton. This Mr. Summers of whom you spoke just now."

"Ah! if I could but think so! but no, I know her faithful heart too well. She will ever consider herself bound to me while I live; my death only can release her, poor darling."

"Don't get such a morbid fancy into your head, Grafton!" answered Saunders, earnestly.

"You need not fear for me," said George, "I am perfectly sane, and I fear God. I am not likely to make away with myself, but I should hail death as the best companion I could meet with. I have lived my life; it can hold nothing for me now but misery; but there may be work for me to do yet. I must wait for this letter which is to tell me all."

Sydney Saunders kept an eye on his

friend. He did not like his melancholy quietness.

The days crept slowly by, lead weighted to George; but however laggard time may seem, it goes surely, marking its flight by days and nights, as it goes to join in the vast circle of eternity.

At last, as it appeared to George, the mortal remains of Dr. Cartland were laid to rest. There had been, after all, but five little days since the love-light had gone out of the eyes that looked on Kate—five days since life had ended for George too. When he found her—his lost wife—found her! but how? Five days of numbness; of dead despair. Had he wished for a divorce from Kate, her insanity would have precluded it. He could never repair the bitter wrong he had done Beryl—his wife—the mother of his only child.

Wherever he looked there was nothing but the blackness of desolation. Nothing could help Kate, her state shut her out from relief of any kind. She was past pity, past love, past blame, past reproach. As dead to him, in her incurable madness, as if she were ten feet underground, with a tombstone as tall as the Monument, or the Tower of Babel!

Beryl then must be his thought, and yet he must never see her again, never look into the pure, clear depths of her love-laughing eyes, never kiss the carnation lips which for him alone had pouted, tempting kisses unawares, never stroke the bright, fair head with its glory of rippling hair, never clasp the fragile form in his arms, never press her to his heart, and hear hers beat for him. She was lost, lost, lost! How cold had been his return for her love, and such love. How unwillingly he had taken her into his life, and having taken her, how she had crept into his heart, warming it with her warmth and life. Still he had kept a chamber in it where Kate yet reigned, and in which there had been no room for the child-wife. But now that she was lost to him, he knew what she had been, what she was to him still—the dearest thing on earth, a ray of light from Heaven, and that life without her would be a dreary business, and yet he *must* so live. Not for the happiness of time and eternity would he add to the wrong he had already done her unknowingly. Poor innocent darling. She would suffer, but it was better for her to suffer than sin! Beryl and purity were synonymous terms in his mind.

Sydney Saunders entered his room according to appointment, and gave George the expected letter, which he opened with trembling hands. It contained a short note and a packet.

The note ran as follows—

"My dear Grafton,—Before you receive this letter I shall have departed out of this world; my time in it is even now short, and while I have still strength I am anxious to confess to you, whom I have injured, how low I have fallen; and yet I would do it all again, and worse, for the happiness the deception has given me.

"Three years of bliss ! If there *be* a God I thank Him for it; if there be a hell I am content to suffer for it. I should die happier if I could have your forgiveness. Much as I have injured you, Grafton, I have liked you better than other men.

"If you can forgive me, do, and do not curse me. My darling is well provided for; she is innocent of all but loving me. If that be guilt, she was guilty; for she loved me with a love equal to my own for her; but she married me, believing you to have been drowned on your passage to Ceylon.

"She was ignorant of all that went before, as the enclosed packet will show.

"You are happy with another wife, Grafton. Be happy still, and leave poor Kate in her present belief that you are dead.

"Good-by, for the last time, George. I wish I had injured any other man than you—but I would not recall it if I could.

"Yours, no more,

"H. CARTLAND."

The letter fell from George's hand.

"Married him, believing me to be dead," he gasped. "Poor Kate! poor, innocent Kate, to have fallen into the hands of such a villain. Saunders," he cried, laying his hand upon his arm, heavily—"Saunders, do you hear? she believed me dead—believed me dead. Oh, my God! that for three years he can have kept up this farce, bringing misery upon the innocent. When I think of Kate, and of Beryl, I feel as if no curses could be too heavy to heap upon the man who has done this thing."

"Grafton," said Mr. Saunders, "the man is dead; he has gone to give an account to a higher power than man's. If you curse him now it can only rebound on your own head; he is past the reach of it. The only thing you could do would be to blacken his memory, and that would be to tell the world of the terrible position in which you are placed; to bring disgrace on the innocent woman who believes herself your wife. Leave the sinner in God's hands, and do your best to shield your poor girl from the knowledge of her position. Plead business, plead illness; make any excuse, but never let her know the real reason of your not returning to her, poor soul. Grafton," said he, after a pause, "so intensely do I feel for your Beryl that if it could be I would make her my wife, and stand by her in her trouble. I have never seen her, but what of that? it would be a thing to be proud of to stand up with such a woman against the world."

George grasped the hand of the lawyer, and answered in a choked voice—

"God reward you, Saunders; and if ever my poor Beryl wants a friend I know she will find one in you. But not while I live will she believe herself free. Beryl, Beryl, my poor child, what can I do with you?"

"You have not read Cartland's confession yet, Grafton," said Sydney Saunders, anxious to call off his attention from the poor girl his love had injured.

"Read it to me," said George; "my eyes are dim."

They were dim; dim with tears for his lost, trusting Beryl; the treasure he might never call his own again as long as he lived.

And the lawyer unfolded and read—

Harry Cartland's Confession to George Grafton.

From the moment I saw your wife as Kate Kerley on your wedding day, I loved her, but I studiously kept the secret of that love from her. She did not love me, and the knowledge of it would insure my dismissal from your house with ignominy. It was, however, happiness enough to see her and to be near her, which our old friendship enabled me to be. She grew to like me—she grew to love me—how gradual it was; but I found it out one glorious evening as she sung.

Oh! how she shrunk from me after that; but I was patient, never scaring her with a look or a word. I was with her daily, and I was content.

Then you went away and left me still free to come and go in your home. How could I who loved her resist any longer. I stayed away and made her feel lonely. Then she protected herself by sending for your sister, and I turned that against her. I used Miss Grafton to make her jealous, to make her acknowledge to herself and me the depth of her love; not for you, her legal husband, but for me—for me. The night before your sister left they both expected I was going to propose to Laura, but I was only maddening Kate. I knew I must madden her before I could make her acknowledge her love for me It was unmanly, but I did it. She left me with Miss Grafton, and I found the *truth* or part of it, was necessary.

I told your sister that I did not mean to marry, and she left me and went to her room. I lingered on, hoping to see Kate, but she never came near me.

At last I strolled into the garden—into the wilderness. There I found her, a white heap prone on the dark damp ground, struggling, struggling with her love for me. I found her thus, and I loved her madly.

Was it likely that I should forego my advantage? Not I. I poured my passionate pleading in words of fire into her ears—into her heart, and I made her confess her love by the violence of mine.

Ah, my darling, how she clung to me. She was mad with the joy of our love. She would have left all for love and me that night, my sweet darling; but your sister was there, and I said we must wait till to-morrow, then I would come for her. What Kate suffered from the time I left her till I saw her again I can imagine, but I cannot explain.

I went to the station thinking it *possible* she might be there with your sister, but if not I felt I should be glad to show Miss Grafton the civility of seeing her off, after which I should know that Kate was alone— alone for me. She had not expected me, as

I saw by the pallor that overspread her face.

The train was gone, and I handed her into my carriage with the determination never to part with her again while she and I both lived. She was ill and trembling, she tried to speak, but with what difficulty the words came.

I drove her to my own house, she was very unwilling to enter it, but I told her I must talk to her, and she said she too had something she must say to me; so she came in, and I had conquered.

I let her and myself in with a private key, no one saw us enter, the carriage had driven round to the stable, and I took her to my private rooms, where I never allowed any foot but my own to enter. I threw my arms about her, how she trembled.

"Kate!" I cried, "mine—mine at last; mine so long as we live—my darling, darling, how I love you!"

I kissed her with untiring lips of passionate entreaty, but she only trembled like a shaken leaf. I held her in my arms, pleading for her consent to stay with me, now and ever. I can see now the deadly struggle that love and duty held within her breast, and then she slipped from my embrace, down, down, down, cowering at my feet, holding them in her agony—her lovely face caressing them.

"I love you!" she cried. "Oh, my God! I say it and live!"

How she writhed in the soul-suffering she went through.

I lifted up my darling and placed her in a chair, and knelt to her, she should not humble herself to me.

"Kate," I said—"Kate, what does this mean? If you love me thus why this bitter grief? Surely we shall be happy—oh, how happy, love!" I cried, triumphantly, holding her dear hands in mine, and looking into the depths of her troubled, glorious eyes.

"Harry," she said, calmly, "I ask your forgiveness for having deceived you. I love you beyond anything and everything on earth, but I am George's wife, and I must be true to my vows to him. My God! I must, I MUST!" she cried, passionately.

"Yet, Kate, you would have come with me last night. What is the difference between last night and to-day? Were you not equally his wife then?" I asked, reproachfully.

"Yes, yes, I know; I am deceitful to you

both, but I was mad then, and now I am sane. Harry!" she cried with excitement, "I suffered the tortures of the damned last night, after you left. You gave me all those hours for reflection, and during them I saw the enormity of the sin I had been so ready to commit. Not only was I on the verge of selling my soul and yours, but of breaking the heart of the truest man ever born of woman. Harry—Harry—I cannot take back my love; that you have, and it is not in my power to take it again, but it is in my power to keep from going utterly to the devil, and taking you with me, and I am determined not to do it. I would rather die."

"And this is your love!" I cried, gazing into the earnest eyes. "This is the love which I believed would surpass the love of all women in the world. Oh! Kate,

Kate!" and I who had never shed a tear in my life, fell into a passion of weeping, shaken by the sobs of despair and cruellest disappointment.

Kate's arms were about me, her lips upon my fevered brow.

"I love you! hush, hush! Harry, hush!"

She soothed me as if I had been a child. Her touch added fuel to fire.

"Kate," I cried, "you shall never leave me—never. I swear it. Love is the only thing that can bind a man to a woman—a woman to a man. We are bound hand and foot, body and soul; we will never part again."

"I must go now," she answered, as if in fear. "Good-by."

She rose and held out her cold hand.

"We will never say that, sweetheart, till either you or I die!" I answered firmly.

"Let me go!" she pleaded.

"Go where, Kate?"

"Home," she answered, trembling.

"My darling, you are at home, and by the God you believe in you shall never leave me for any other," and I left the room, carefully locking it after me, to go and see for some dinner for my darling. I must get it from a pastrycook's and bring it in myself, so as to arouse no suspicion in the minds of the servants. There was no bell in the room. Kate could not call for assistance, and the suite of rooms were lighted from the roof. She was safe, and undoubtedly mine. Just as I was leaving the house Fate put into my hand a tool which made it easy for me to keep Kate without suspicion. There was an earnest request that I should hurry out to see a young woman who had been taken very ill, and was now in a cab outside. I went to see her at once, and found that she was in a dying state from congestion of the lungs.

It was evident that the girl had a history, but she would not tell me a word of it, and answered my questions with pain and difficulty. She said she had no home and nowhere to go, and asked if I would give her an order of admission to one of the hospitals. She had dark hair, dark eyes, and small features, not unlike Kate's, and was about her height, but she was older and thinner; still the likeness tempted me. I told her I would take her to a respectable lodging I knew of, and getting into the cab with her I bade the man drive to Kentish Town, trusting to luck for what I wanted.

Yes, that would do, and I stopped the cab and went in, and had a talk to the landlady. She was very needy, and not very inquisitive. She undertook to nurse the young lady, and helped her in. I knew she could not recover. I knew, also, that whoever she was, she meant to keep her secret, for she would give me no clue to it. This was Saturday. I paid the landlady well, and she did all she could for the dying woman, but nothing could save her.

I went back to Kate, took her dinner to her myself, and did my best to make her comfortable. She sat by the fireplace, silently looking at the empty hearth, her hands lying feebly in her lap. She only spoke to me once—she asked me to let her go home. I told her I had telegraphed to her servants that she was too unwell to return, and that she would remain with friends for a day or two. She looked up at me.

"I am unwell, Dr. Cartland. This will kill me; let me go home."

It was all in vain.

"I am going to kill you, Kate," I laughed, "in a way you little dream of."

Even she smiled, never for a second imagining what I meant—how should she?—smiled at the idea of my killing her. I did my best to make her happy and comfortable.

"Kate," I said, straining her unwilling form to my breast, "I will never ask you to be a wife to me till you can tell me you stay of your own free will."

"And that will never be while *George lives!* Harry, be content with my love; ask no more of me, I can be no more to you. It is not too late even now; let me go, love, don't keep me like a caged bird, or I may learn to hate you. Come and see me as you used to do. I can't live quite without you, dear, but don't disgrace me before all the world. Don't, Harry—don't.

I could not bear it," lifting tearful eyes to mine. " You may keep me here a year—two—ten—but I can never be more to you than I am now," she cried, with flushed cheeks.

" Very well, Kate, so be it; but if you knew that George was dead, how soon then would you become my wife?" grasping her arm tightly, and awaiting her reply.

" You wouldn't kill him!" she gasped, with dilated nostrils and wide-open eyes, like a frightened horse.

" Kill him! bah, child—no! Come, tell me how soon ?"

" When I cease to be his I am yours, love," she answered, earnestly. " While he lives—NEVER !"

I kissed and left her, then sent a " commissionaire" down to Hazelhurst for some clothes for her, and took them to her when they arrived. The next day the stranger-woman died. In her extremity I sent for another doctor whom I knew slightly—Dr. Duval, a man who had lived abroad all his days, and we were both with her when life ceased. Then I had the body dressed in one of Kate's night-dresses, which I had abstracted from the bag her maid had sent from Hazelhurst.

On Monday I ordered the coffin. On Tuesday I took her down there as your wife, and buried her by her name. I had noticed the scratch on Kate's arm—I made one on that of the dead woman, in case of any investigation.

Miss Ansell suspected me, but she could prove nothing, and the body was sworn to by Kate's own maid.

Great was my relief when the funeral was over. A week I had kept my darling under lock and key, still she was obdurate, shrinking from me. My love had made no way with her—she was faithful to you, George.

On the Saturday morning I opened my newspaper and read—

"Loss of the 'May Queen,' and all hands on board!"

How eagerly I scanned this short notice. The "May Queen" was supposed to have struck on the Maldive Rocks. A vessel had picked up some timber bearing her name, and that was all that was left to tell the tale of this dreadful loss of life and property.

The quick blood rushed through my veins, and crushing the paper into my pocket I walked up to Kate's rooms. She was sitting listlessly as usual, and hardly looked up as I entered.

"Kate," I said, my heart knocking hard against my ribs—"Kate," I said, with subdued passion, "you told me the other day that if you were free you would be mine at once, did you not?"

"I did, Harry, and I repeat it; but I am not free, and you are bringing ruin and disgrace on me by detaining me here."

Her lips trembled painfully, and she clasped and unclasped her hands—too nervous to keep still.

"My darling!" I cried, "you are free; come, come to me!"

She sprang from her chair, a look of horror was on her face. She caught blindly at something to support her, and asked with trembling—

"George—is——?"

I finished the sentence for her—"DEAD! Yes, Kate, drowned; the 'May Queen' has gone down with all hands on board."

She sunk back into her chair—dazed. She passed her restless hand across her brow again and again. After awhile she asked to see the paper herself, and then without another word she came and put her arms about my neck.

"My love can hurt no one now, dear. I am yours now poor George has gone. Tell me you love me, Harry, or my heart will break."

My answer was to pour out upon her the pent-up passion of my soul. Now then, at last, she was truly mine. She had given herself up to me quivering in response to my wild embraces. Oh, how I loved her. Before noon next day she was my wife. We were married by special licence, with no one to witness to the validity of the marriage but the clergyman, the clerk, and the old woman who cleaned the church. They managed everything between them, and I took my dear wife straight away to Dover, and thence to the Continent, to travel, for she had altered sadly during that one week I held her in captivity. And then for me there came an awakening. We were married, and Kate was unknowingly a bigamist. You still lived. You had been saved, I found, with others, from the wreck. To tell Kate this would have been to lose her, and worse than that to cause her the most fearful remorse and misery. All believed her dead. It was impossible for her to return to her old home, or to your relations. I watched over her, allowing neither people nor papers to come near her, till I feared the complete loss of my practice unless I looked after it a little. I had left Duval to attend to it. When we had been married three months I took Kate home. We lived at an hotel till I found "The Nook," where I settled with my darling happily. She grieved for you as for a lost brother, but gave me all the love and worship of her woman's heart. Poor Kate, my wish was law to her. I begged her never to go out anywhere without me, and she obeyed me to the letter. Ours was perfect love and complete happiness. She never knew of your rescue, never knew of your marriage, to the girl with the romantic name which I forget. If she ever hears of one or the other, George, it will break her heart. Remember she was true to you in temptation, and spare her. No one but you and Saunders need ever know of this, and he has promised to befriend my darling. I alone am to blame. Kate is innocent. He will take care this reaches you, and if you wisely decide to remain in Ceylon no unpleasant revelations can ever be made to your wife. Women are apt to try and discover your secrets if they think there is any mystery.

"H. CARTLAND.

"June, 187 ."

The lawyer and the client sat silent after the above revelation. What was there to say? The sinner was dead. The sinned against suffering. The former was beyond the reach of punishment, the latter was past the hope of help. Then there came to George the remembrance of that text which before he had never seen much sense in—"Thy strength shall be to sit still."

CHAPTER VIII.

MISS ANSELL DOES HER DUTY.

GEORGE GRAFTON had an interview with Miss Ansell. She was Kate's only relation, and he thought, hard as she was, she would be moved to pity, and he was right.

He felt that the sight of him could only make Kate more violent, believing him to be an avenging spirit. He longed much to take her in his arms, and to give her one kiss of forgiveness, but feared the sight of him would harm her. He told Miss Ansell his sad story word for word, and asked her advice.

Never before had the austere old woman

been overtaken by weakness. But now tears chased each other down her wrinkled cheeks and she kissed George! and told him that never from *her* lips should any one hear of the mystery that had overshadowed his life!

She offered to receive Kate and a woman-keeper, and promised to see that she was treated with care and kindness, and then she asked in a troubled voice about Beryl, and George told her that he was going to keep her in the dark as long as possible, but that he would not return to her.

He confessed that he had not made up his mind what he should do yet, but that he had decided he and Beryl must never meet again; and Miss Ansell, grasping his hand, blinked away her tears to look at him, for, as she remarked, he was the first good man she had met with in the course of her long life.

So they agreed that the secret should rest with those three (themselves, and Mr. Saunders), not even Dr. Grafton was to know of the sad trouble that had fallen on George— his son.

Kate was once more received under her aunt's roof.

The old woman had prepared for her a suite of newly chintzed rooms, and the poor maniac had settled down to her objectless life.

She was seldom violent, but utterly listless. Her love of flowers seemed all that was left to her of the past. Memory appeared to have failed. At times, if anything reminded her of her lost love, she broke out. The tolling of a bell drove her frantic, but she had not the reason to tell you why.

She became a shadow of the Kate of olden times—beautiful still, but sad to look upon. There was now no sense in the large dark eyes that looked so unnaturally big in her pale sunken face.

Anything pretty attracted her, as if she were still a child.

Miss Ansell had a liberal allowance with her, and did all in her power to make her happy; bought her flowers and fruits, and all the things she showed any pleasure in. She drove or walked daily with her attendant, and on one of these excursions took a fancy to a small dog at a cottage door. The dog was something for her to love, and the poor unreasoning creature clung to it wildly, crying if it were taken out of her sight.

Everything went on quietly in the old maid's establishment. Kate had her dog and was happy; the past being mercifully hidden from her.

Kate's money made Miss Ansell's circumstances easy; not that she would have hesitated to receive her great niece if she had been penniless, for she considered it her duty. And George had gone home to stay with his parents. The strain upon his nerves at last had worn him nearly out. His father feared brain fever, and called in fresh advice; it proved to be but too true, and George Grafton lay between life and death.

Mrs. Grafton, not knowing her son's sad secret, did the one thing which in all the world he would have wished her to leave undone—she wrote and told Beryl.

CHAPTER IX.

HOPES AND FEARS.

GEORGE had tender nurses in his mother and sisters, but the grim scythe-bearer was strong, and he, worn out with trouble and sickness, was very weak, but fought every inch of ground manfully, amidst the hopes and fears of his relations.

If he had had happiness and love to live for, he could not have made a harder struggle of it, and at last he got the upper hand, and was pronounced out of danger.

Then, week by week, day by day, he dragged on wearily the long hours of weakness, strengthening as slowly as the lengthening light of Spring's earliest days.

And all the time Beryl and her child are coming—coming, as fast as they can.

When little Beryl got her mother-in-law's letter, she was beside herself with grief; but directly she saw that it was her duty to go to him, she roused herself to action, packed up and started, as if she were accustomed to life's buffets.

Ah! the hopes and fears of that loving heart. Each oscillation of the screw throbbed to some troubled thought of George; Even the horror of being again on shipboard was lost in the agony of her mind to see him once more, to know that he still lived and loved her.

It was so far off! such a long way to go to him—might he not be worse before she reached England? shivering and awe-stricken, she asked herself. Might he not be dead! dead! dead!

She strained her eyes for the white cliffs of Albion—her sinking heart sick with suspense. How should she find him? alive or dead?

At anchor at last! Such a scene of confusion, that small Beryl is bewildered utterly —the steam is being let off with deafening noise and blinding mist. A thick November fog lies dark and heavy upon land and sea. Eager faces looking out for friends on shore, hidden by the thickness of the atmosphere. Sailors and passengers hurrying to and fro, luggage bumping and banging on the deck, cries of porters and hotel-touters on the quay, greeting of acquaintances, faces bright with happiness, faces blank with disappointment, faces flushed with expectancy, faces pinched by sorrow, faces blue with cold, all—all—going on shore; and among them Beryl and her boy, and no one has come to meet her.

She feels this with a sense of blankness— of disappointment, and puts it away with impatience.

How should they know she was coming? Of course they couldn't, it was absurd of her to have expected it; and she hurried to the station, and on again to find George, and there she is at last at Dr. Grafton's door, with panting heart and small worn-out body, inquiring for Mr. George Grafton!

"Mr. George was better," the servant said, looking curiously at the agitated face before him—"better, and out of danger, but very weak!"

And poor Beryl, the strain taken off which had held her nerves at tightest tension for so long, collapsed, and would have fallen to the ground but for the strong arms of the servant, which found no difficulty in supporting the little body and carrying her into his master's surgery.

Beryl was not expected. How were the Graftons to know that she would undertake such a weary journey all alone. They did not know the girl, and her loving heart, or they might have done so; and to their surprise George had never mentioned her to them, and if they brought her name on the tapis, he shrank with such visible pain from the subject, that they were not inclined to care for the small creature, and were surprised (not pleasantly) to learn that a little woman with a fine baby—a servant—and numerous large boxes had arrived, and that the former was lying insensible in the surgery.

Dr. Grafton, however, went to her at once,

and looking on her still, sweet face, confessed to himself it was angelic, and fell in love with her on the spot.

It was not long before the blue eyes unclosed to look at him, and he leaned over the girl and told her who he was, and she gave him two little hands and called him "Father."

She entreated to be allowed to go at once to her husband—it would be such a pleasant surprise for him.

Dr. Grafton said that George was asleep.

"Oh!" cried Beryl, "I will not disturb him; I will creep in so quietly, and sit beside him; and when he wakes he will find me there."

Dr. Grafton smiled. He would rather his son had been told of the advent of his wife; but he had not the heart to cause a cloud on the eager little face, turned up to him so confidingly, and he did not believe a joyful shock would hurt any one. So Beryl had her way; and after being introduced to her new relations, and leaving them "baby" to amuse, she crept, with gentle feet to her husband's door, into the room, gazed upon the sleeping face with an intense longing to run and kiss her darling, resisted the innocent temptation, and seated herself beside the bed, almost hidden by the curtains which hung from the Arabian top; and from there she watched the dear face. How altered it was! altered and pain-stricken.

What he must have suffered, to have brought such lines and care-marks on the brow that was so placid, and in her grief for his sufferings, a slight cry escaped her lips. His name, uttered with such gentleness and sorrow, such tender passion and compassion. It was so soft, it might have been breathed by some being from another world; but, slight as the sound was, it had aroused him; or perhaps it was the unknown influence merely of Beryl's presence. But George stirred, moved uneasily, and repeated, in a tone of such unutterable anguish—

"Lost—lost, lost! Beryl, my little Beryl, lost, lost—lost!"

"Oh, George," cried the small wife, "wake, love, wake!"

Better to wake than to dream such dreams, she thought, as she rose and bent over him, looking at the horror of his awakened face.

"George," she pleaded, "I am not lost. I am here, my love. I am here with you, and I will never leave you again."

For one moment his face lighted up as with sunshine, and he held out his eager arms to clasp her; but before she had time to shelter there, he dropped them, with an exceeding bitter cry—

"Never again, while I live!" and lay in a stupor as of death.

"Father in Heaven," prayed Beryl, sinking on her knees, "give him back to me, and show me how to comfort him."

And then she rang the bell, and loving faces gathered round the bed. Beryl stood there, white and motionless.

Dr. Grafton whispered—

"It was mad of me to let you go to him; the shock has been too much."

But George Grafton pulled through, and again awoke to find his wife by his side, with painful pleasure; lying quietly with a half-smile, while she caressed him, wondering, oh! how she wondered, that he gave her no welcome, that she was not asked into his arms to nestle there.

And then she brought the boy, and at sight of him George's breast swelled convulsively, and Beryl's gentle heart was torn by his sobs of agony, and she gently, but firmly, took him in her arms.

"George," she said, "you are in some trouble, this is not the effect of illness. I am your wife, and I have the right to share it, and share it I will."

"Beryl," he moaned, "I *am* in trouble, bitterest, sorest trouble; but I cannot tell it to you. It would break your heart, as it has done mine," and then, after a pause, he broke out, passionately, "for the love of God, leave me, Beryl; leave me, and let me never look upon your face again. Oh, my darling, my darling! I am weak. It drives me mad to see you by me, and know that to clasp you to my heart would be a sin. Help me, Beryl! help me! be brave, and go away while there is yet time, before I yield to this cruel temptation to hold by you, in defiance of the laws of God and man. Go, child, go; you cannot, must not, stay here."

She looked at him, with despair gnawing at her heart. Was he mad? her love, her darling, her own dear husband, that he should wish to send her from him. His little Beryl, his loving wife! White as death, she stood looking at him; her blue eyes all pupil, and darkness in the horror of her gaze, her small hands clasped and locked, as if she were struggling for life.

George saw her soul's suffering, and crying—

"Once more, love!" he drew her to him eagerly, and held her to his heart in a passionate embrace. "May God bless you, dear one, and protect you from harm. Now go and ask my father to come to me. I want to talk to him alone."

"Alone? Without me?" she asked, lifting her wondering eyes to his.

"Yes; without you, little one. Beryl, I must learn to do without you."

"It wont be for long, George. How long will this talk last? ten minutes? If you are more, I shall come back!"

And she left him with a smile—a smile called to her lips by the renewed pressure of the arms that had clasped her so tenderly, though with such wild words—and she sought her father-in-law, half in joy, half sorrow, and when she had found him, she seated herself at his feet, and took possession of his hands, and looked up, with affectionate confidence, in his face.

"Father, George's father, you wouldn't deceive me, would you?"

"Deceive you, child; indeed I would not. Who could look into your trusting face and do so? No one, surely."

"I am so glad you like me," she said, with a half-shy smile of pleasure. "Will you please tell me what brought on George's illness?"

"I cannot do that child, for it has been a puzzle to me."

"Father," said Beryl, putting one hand impressively on his arm. "You—you don't think," hesitating between each word, "that—that he is mad!"

"Good heavens, child, mad! such a thing as madness has never been heard of in our family. Mad, indeed. He has of course been delirious. Brain fever is no joke, I can assure you; but all his painful fancies have left him with returning health. He will be able to take you about soon again, my dear, and you will find him sane enough, I'll warrant."

"And yet," said Beryl simply, while tears stood in her eyes, "he has been asking me to go away and leave him, and never to let him see me any more. I love him so, that it is hard to bear," her tears falling silently and fast, "and yet he clasped me to him as if it were pain to part with me. Oh! he *does* love me—he does, he does."

Dr. Grafton regarded her pityingly.

"You have vexed him child, run, tell him you are sorry, and he will soon dry those tears, or I am not acquainted with my son," he said with an honest laugh. "Lovers' quarrels are soon mended little Beryl."

"Dr. Grafton," she said earnestly, "George and I have never, never, had a quarrel in our lives, never one word of disagreement."

Her father-in-law looked at her and kissed her forehead.

"Beryl," he said, "I feel sure, at any rate, you are in no way to blame."

"Thank you," she answered; "and now I must deliver you George's message. He wishes to see you at once, and I am not to be present;" but I shall not be very patient, and if you don't call me soon I shall come without."

And Beryl slid away quietly, leaving Dr. Grafton free to answer his son's summons.

"I can't understand it," he muttered—"I can't understand it. An angel for a wife, a cherub for a son, a good income, and yet the lad is miserable, broken-hearted. What can it all mean—poor George."

In another minute he was in his son's

room, looking into his pale, agitated face, "You sent for me, George?"

"Yes, father."

Dr. Grafton sat down beside him.

"George, you are weak and ill, and I fear give way to nervous fancies. You have scared poor little Beryl out of her wits. What have you said to her?"

"Father," said George, "I have tried to bear the burden alone, but it has got beyond me, I must now have your help and advice. If Beryl had not come home it might have been kept secret. Oh, why did she come—why did she come?"

"Because," said Dr. Grafton, regarding him gravely—"because she valued you, George, more than you seem to value her; because she knew you were ill, and because she is your wife."

"Oh, God!" cried George, "that is the

bitterness of it, she is not my wife—my God, she is not!" looking with despair into the blank dismay of his father's face.

"Not your wife?" said Dr. Grafton; "do I hear you aright? George!"

"You do, indeed."

"Then George," cried the old man, rising in agitation, "you — you are—a scoundrel. Such a child—so sweetly innocent. My God! I can't believe that a son of mine could be so dastardly a coward. It is impossible, George. You must be mad!"

"Likely enough," answered he sadly. "I have had enough to make me so, but I sent for you, sir, to ask your help, not to hear your reproaches. May God judge me if I have wilfully wronged Beryl. She is all you say, and more; my greatest sin against her was not giving her such a wealth of

love as she has bestowed upon me; but I
have loved before, and she had not. Still
I made her my wife honestly, intending to
make her happy, and I think I succeeded."

"For Heaven's sake, George, recollect
yourself. A moment ago you said she was
not your wife, and now you say you made
her your wife. What do you mean?"

"Both things are true," said George, "I
did make her so, believing myself free to do
it, but I was not. *Kate is alive*, and Beryl
is not my wife."

Dr Grafton staggered like one drunk.
The father and son talked long and earnestly
over the sad case, tried to hit upon any plan
by which Beryl might be spared the knowledge of the cruel position in which she
was placed; but no such plan was feasible,
Such a woman as George's wife could not be
put off with an excuse. She would never

consent to leave him while she believed herself to be his wife. She must be told *the truth*, whatever the consequences might be—*the truth*, the *whole truth*, and *nothing but the truth!*

George told his father the whole story, which Dr. Cartland's confession had put him in possession of, and now it had all to be told again, for Beryl was at the door, asking to come in.

"It is better so," said Dr. Grafton, " better got over at once."

And Beryl came in, and standing between the two looked first at one pale face and then at the other, speechless, not knowing what she had to fear.

CHAPTER X.

BERYL'S CHOICE.

"BERYL," said Dr. Grafton, tenderly leading her to a chair, "we are in great trouble; will you try not to add to it, child—by being brave?"

"Yes" (with trembling wonder). "If it is anything very, very bad, let me hold George's hand."

And he stretched it out to her at once.

"George, will you tell her, or shall I?" said the old man, shrinking from the painful task.

"I cannot," answered George, pitifully.

"Oh, go on!" said Beryl; "what—what is it?"

"Little Beryl," said Dr. Grafton, "you love George, and would do anything to save him pain; from more pain than is necessary."

"I love him," answered Beryl, with bright, eager eyes, "and would do anything to save him pain!"

"Then listen, dear child. If after a year and more of married life, George had found that—that—there had been a flaw in the legality of your marriage, you would be sensible, and not distress him by asking him to continue those ties unlawfully, however much he might love you, would you not, little Beryl?"

She grew whiter than a snowdrop, standing with bent neck, meekly by.

"I would ask him," she answered, while her cheeks flushed with excitement—"I would ask him to send for a clergyman, and marry me at once—again; that there might be no flaw. I would ask him, because flaw or no flaw, I am his wife before God!"

Then silence, broken by George.

"But darling! if it was worse than a flaw, an obstacle—an obstacle which no human power could remove, what would you do then?"

"I would pray to God, and He would remove it," she answered, with earnest solemnity.

"Beryl, Beryl, it is now as it was when I talked to you that day before we were married. Do you remember?" cried George, in an agony.

"Yes, I remember, you said you were going to leave me, and I said I would follow you wherever you went."

"Yes, love! and I gave way to you, little dreaming of the misery which I should cause you, and now the time has come, my darling, when we must part."

"Part," cried Beryl, with defiant misery, "you cannot send me from you now, for *now* I am your wife."

"Would to God that you were, Beryl—my little love! try, try, for my sake, to bear it, you are not my wife, my poor darling *Kate is alive.*"

Beryl uttered no cry, shed no tear, she threw out her arms, as if to ward off the blow with her tiny hands, but all so silently, so sadly. She looked all the time at George like a somnambulist, making no sign of her suffering.

"Do you understand me, little love?"

"I believe so;" she answered, "I am not really your wife! she did not die after all."

"Yes, that is it, love! and my Beryl sees that she must try and make herself happy away from me." George's voice trembled ominously.

"George," she said, gathering herself together, "are you going back to—to her?"

"No, no, my precious darling."

"George," she went on, "do you still love me?"

"My darling," he cried, passionately, "God knows I love you, I never knew how dearly, till I had lost you! You are dearer to me than all the world beside, little one!"

"And you are dearer to me than all the world, George," with a fine smile, drawing up her slender neck. "I choose *you* in preference to the world!"

"Beryl," said Dr. Grafton, "you are too innocent to understand, but believe me you cannot continue in your present position, as George's supposed wife."

The girl looked at him unflinchingly.

"Why?"

"Good heavens, child! how, how can I answer you?" he cried impatiently; "you don't know what the world would say of you."

"Let the world say what it likes, I will never leave George while he and I live. I will be to him whatever he likes, his wife still if he will, his companion, his friend, his servant, but when you ask me to leave him, I say never, never."

"George," said Dr. Grafton, "perhaps your mother can explain to her better than we can how impossible such an arrangement would be," and he left the room to seek his wife.

Beryl threw herself on George's breast.

"George," she moaned, "if you send me from you, I shall die!"

"But, my little Beryl, you would not wish to stay with me if it were wrong—a sin?"

"It has not been a sin up to now, love. How can it be more a sin than it has been?"

"Beryl," said George, with a shade of impatience, "you are a perfect child still!"

"And you wont send me away, dearest, will you?" asked the girl, stroking his haggard face.

"Beryl! Beryl! for God's sake don't tempt me," cried the man, trembling with the excitement he endeavoured to calm, and Beryl trembled too—trembled with pleasure that he still loved her so—trembled with fear lest he should send her from him— trembled that for love she could give up right, but never swerved from her decision.

"George," she said solemnly, "it cannot be wrong to love as I love you. God would not plant such undying affection in my heart just for it to wither and die; if we married not knowing there was a barrier between us, the fault was not ours, it does not release us from our vows. George, we cannot part! what would become of me? what would become of baby if you forsake us?" she pleaded earnestly.

George did not answer for some time. A passionate war was raging in his heart—this little wife of his! how could he give her up? how could he break her gentle spirit and kill her confiding love? She would learn to hate him if he sent her from him, and how could she buffet with the world alone, with no strong arm to protect her. O God! and what would his life be without her, with no one to love him, no one to love. The temptation was very strong.

"Beryl," he cried passionately—"Beryl, can you sin for me—can you meet with scorn for me—be looked upon as a vile thing among men and women for my sake—be an outcast from society and lose your self-respect, all—all, for me?"

She looked at him with a pale, firm face; the blood had forsaken her lips, but she trembled no longer.

"Yes, George, I can and will."

"Then may God help you, child, and forgive me," he cried, gathering her to him with hungry eagerness.

This was Beryl's choice.

CHAPTER XI.

GONE!

MRS. GRAFTON spoke seriously to Beryl, and did all she could to break the resolution she had formed to stand by her son, but all her talk availed nothing. The girl was gentle, but as firm as a rock. Dr. Grafton said a great deal to George, but his own conscience said more; he had ever been in every sense of the word, an honourable man, and now he told himself he was on the verge of becoming a scoundrel!

If a pure innocent creature like Beryl was willing to sully her purity and innocence for him because of her deep love for him, surely he ought to be man enough to shield her from herself, and from the sin and its consequences that her devotion would bring upon her.

It was so sweet to think of having her by his side through life, that the battle was a hard one, but George's good angel won the victory, and though he knew what a blank his life would be from henceforth, he decided to save Beryl in spite of herself, and he felt more at peace than he had done since he had received Miss Ansell's letter in Ceylon, which overshadowed him with the cloud of the terrible mystery which had since come to light.

George had a long confidential talk with his father, and the upshot of it was, that George was to go away without anybody knowing where, except his father, and Beryl was still to be called "Mrs. George," and was to remain with her child as a daughter, under the doctor's roof. This would shield her from any remarks that might otherwise be made by good-natured Mrs. Grundy.

By this arrangement Beryl would not be lonely, and would be safe from all harm.

So George was content to go and bear the burden alone. He was now strong enough to be out and about. He had retained his little bachelor room in which he had slept in his childhood, while Beryl and her boy occupied grander quarters, but she used to run to his door, clad in her pale blue dressing gown, to inquire for him every morning directly she got up.

On the morning after the above-named conversation between father and son, there was no response to her knock, no answer to her loving words.

"Was he asleep? was he ill? was he dead?" she asked herself, while a great trembling seized her limbs, and her tongue was silent from fear. He always locked the door, so she could not get in! and then she turned the handle, and to her surprise it opened.

With dread she glanced into the room, and spoke—still no answer, no sound. She crept on with uncertain, wavering steps, but still no sign of life. She turned to look at the bed with a chill horror, and saw with a sense of relief that he was not there. Where was he? She supposed that he must be up and gone down; perhaps she was late, had overslept herself.

Dear George! she would lay her head on his pillow just where he had lain, and a smile of love took a quick flight across her pale face—pale and delicate, and pure as an early snowdrop—but it did not last long. She saw, while a spasm of apprehensive fear contracted her heart, that the bed had not been slept in, that drawers were open, clothes evidently selected from, while others were left in untidy heaps; all the débris was there which a man always leaves in packing up. It came upon her painfully and slowly, as she looked round the disordered room, that George was gone!

Gone! gone where? Gone from her! and the blankness of despair settled down upon her as she repeated that one word which to her meant so much. Gone!

And there they found her listlessly sitting on the ground, while her bright head rested on some of the clothes George had left.

Her large eyes had grown hollow and weary, even in that short time, and as she lifted her face she only repeated "Gone!"

CHAPTER XII.

DEAD!

HEN George Grafton left his father's house it was with an aching void in his heart. Conscience told him he was right to go away, but his heart clung to Beryl and his boy, and the struggle to leave them was indeed a hard one. The old affection for Kate too was still in his heart, but he knew now he would not reinstate her as his wife if he could, and he was almost distracted with conflicting emotions. Who, after all, could have blamed him if he had taken his little Beryl again into his bosom, and carried her back to her happy home in the bright island of Ceylon? Who,

indeed, George knew who, and went upon his way. Will he lose his reward?

George Grafton went to London, and then took chambers, and began business again. He worked hard, and succeeded in all he undertook. Miss Ansell wrote to him from time to time, with accounts of Kate. She had become very weak and delicate, but seemed to be fast regaining her reason. She had begged Miss Ansell most earnestly to tell her the whole story of the Mystery in which she found herself enveloped, but that good woman would tell her nothing till she had written to ask George's permission, which he gave, and then at last Kate knew all—knew that she had never legally been Harry Cartland's wife—knew that the man she had loved so madly and so blindly had deceived her, had sacrificed her to his ungovernable passion; and her heart yearned towards her noble-minded George, with the sickening knowledge which had come too late to her, how far better *he* would have loved and cared for her if she had but bestowed on him one-tenth of the devotion she had given to Harry Cartland. She might still have been a happy, honoured wife, while now! and she shuddered to think of the present.

She thought of George, and of his goodness, and learnt to love him with a perfect love, made up of respect, affection, and earnest repentance, such a love as she might offer to her God. Very different from the passion-tossed, insane love she had given the man who had ruined her.

Her heart still beat wildly when she thought of him. She would never curse him for his treachery, but she, a dying woman, now gave her new-born purer love to the husband she had wronged and lost. She never tired of talking of him to her aunt, and of the Beryl to whom he had transferred the treasure which in her blindness she had thrown from her.

She thought of her rival with no enmity. Kate, with all her faults, was a noble woman still. Her greatest wish was that Beryl should make her husband happy when she was gone—gone, perhaps, to join the man for whom she had sacrificed all, and who she could now see had been far from perfect, although she had set him up as an idol, and in her ignorance how she had worshipped him!

Thus in her last days Kate saw her sin, and repented of it to her God, and found peace, but of George she had as yet asked no forgiveness, nor of Beryl, whom she had, though unknowingly, injured so deeply.

Her anxiety upon this point hurried her onward to the grave already yawning for her.

One Sunday, looking in her doctor's kindly face, she begged to know the truth, how long she had to live? and he had broken to her gently that the next "Lord's Day" she would spend with *Him*, and weary, world-worn Kate heard him with a smile. Peace at last! peace, after all the sin, all the sorrow, all the suffering. Peace —peace for her!

But Kate, unforgiven Kate, could find no rest. She had not asked and received forgiveness of the husband she had injured, nor of innocent Beryl. With much heart-sickness she confided her trouble to Miss Ansell, and she, ever ready to do her duty, and much softened since first we met her set off at once, to see Beryl, then George.

When Beryl first realised that George for conscience' sake had forsaken her, it nearly broke her heart, but George's son was still at hand to take her out of herself. *He* must not see her cry—baby George's mother must find a smile for George's boy. Thus Beryl—broken-hearted Beryl—learnt to smile again.

Many months had passed since George had left her. The Old Year King had passed away, and given up his sceptre to his successor, who was in full swing of Nature's brightest time—youth!

Spring had come for Beryl as for all the world, a time of cheering sounds, sweet fresh scents and brightest tints, and though she was still very sad, she gladdened under the influence of the joyous season. Still she had not heard once from George. The one and only letter she had ever received from him was worn from constant reading. She kept it in her bosom, and when alone she would read it again and yet again. How happy it had made her; how she had danced for joy, and told her glad news to her unconscious babe upon her knee, to the very walls, tables, and chairs, and still she read the promise that he would come, and tried to fancy it was yet to be fulfilled, and so took comfort.

Miss Ansell reached Worham and had an interview with Beryl. She had not seen her before, and was much taken with her gentle and retiring manner. She was no " Girl of the Period," as the good woman remarked, but one who even our much-lauded grandmothers might have been proud of—and so they might indeed.

When Beryl heard of Kate's wish for forgiveness, and that her end was so near, she begged to be allowed to go to her at once, that she might cheer the last hours of the poor soul, who had sinned, sorrowed, and suffered. Beryl was not one to "pass by on the other side." So this sweet little Samaritan set off on her errand ot mercy without delay, while Miss Ansell went on to London to seek George. To Beryl it was a trial to leave her boy, but ever thinking of others, she would not take him, lest it should bring a pang of sorrow to the childless woman to see her bonny boy, George's little son; and with tender heart she told herself Kate's life might have been different if she had been so blessed, knowing what her child had been to her in her time of trial. Kate's had come and found her all alone, no husband's strong hand to hold her back as she slid almost imperceptibly down-hill.

With such gentle thoughts little Beryl reached Maidenhead and Miss Ansell's trim cottage, made brighter for poor Kate than it had ever been before through the spinster's long life.

Kate was lying on a couch beside the window, dressed in her favourite white, relieved with crimson, looking wondrous handsome with the sun's rays playing about her. Her clear white skin was lit up by a hectic flush on either cheek, and her dark eyes were bright, and looked unnaturally large.

To Beryl's tap, there was a faint "Come in," and George's two wives met.

Each looked at the other earnestly, but although Kate saw the fairy-like little creature before her, and gazed upon her as a lovely vision too bright for a being of this world, she did so with admiration and pleasure, never for a moment dreaming who her visitor was. While Beryl, face to face with George's legal wife, advanced with trembling, hesitating steps, wondering no longer that he had so loved this woman— glorious, even still, with Death's dark hand upon her.

"Kate," she said, timidly, "I have come to nurse you. Will you have me?"

The sick woman smiled happily.

"Who would refuse so good an offer? Where have you come from, child? Earth, or heaven?"

"I have come from Worham, Kate," said Beryl.

A shadow crossed Kate's face.

"From Worham! I too have been there, the name reminds me of a sad past. My parents were both killed there, little fairy."

"Oh, I am so sorry!" said Beryl, nervously; "I ought to have known."

"Known, how should you know, child? You lovely little creature, I wonder if ever you will suffer too—suffer, ay, and sin?"

Beryl took a chair beside the couch, and sat down.

"You seem to think I am a child," she said, sadly; "but I am not. I am not many years younger than yourself, and as for suffering, I have suffered too: like yourself, I lost both my parents together, they were drowned. I thought then every other grief through life must be small to me after that; but I have felt my other trial even more than that. So you see, Kate, I have suffered too. As for sin," a hot blush dyeing her snowy cheek—"I *wished* to sin, and should have done so, but for the self-denial of a noble man!"

Kate was watching her with varying colour.

"Oh, I am so glad you have come, dear fairy! you seem to bring a purer atmosphere with you. And may I tell you my sad story?"

"I know it," said Beryl, "that is why I came. I thought I might be able to comfort you."

"You know it!" cried Kate. "How?"

"Miss Ansell told me," answered Beryl.

"My aunt! I thought she was too kind to talk about me," said Kate, sadly; "but never mind, tell me about the noble-hearted man who saved you. Did you love him, fairy?"

"Yes, yes, indeed I did?"

"*Who was he?*" cried Kate, the hectic spots deepening on her thin cheeks.

"He was your husband," said Beryl, simply, "George Grafton."

"And you are——?" gasped Kate.

"I am Beryl," she answered, gently.

Kate hid her face in her hands. It had been a shock to her to find this beautiful child-like creature was her successor. A spasm of almost jealousy contracted her heart, and left her white, deathly white; but her true nature soon reasserted itself, and she was able to see how good, unselfish, and perfect a woman, this girl must be, who could put her own feelings aside, and come to her, who had been the first cause of her great affliction.

At last Kate emerged from her hand's imprisonment, pale and calm.

"Beryl, may I call you Beryl, you are an angel, and God will reward you for your goodness by the best reward you can have on earth, a good man's love. As for George," she cried, with excitement, "he is a king among men; where could you find his fellow? I tell you, child, nowhere. I threw the treasure of his love from me. I gave up reality for a shadow; but oh, Beryl, it was such a bright shadow; and I did love Harry with such a passionate love! a love that such a gentle nature as yours would not comprehend, Beryl."

"And yet," she answered, her face rosy red with proud shame—"and yet I offered to stay with George, after I knew I was not his wife."

"You did?" cried Kate; and crimson Beryl nodded an affirmative. "Then you are but a woman, after all, like myself," said Kate, with a sigh and a smile; "and I thought George had secured an angel for his second wife."

"I am not his wife," answered the girl, with trembling lips.

Kate took her into her arms and kissed her.

"Poor child! poor child! how you have suffered; but it wont be for long, now dear, only a few short days, and George will be free—free to make you all his own, Beryl, and then you will be so happy, it will make up for past sorrow;" and the fair face brightened at her words.

"You think he will come back, Kate?" she asked.

"I know it," Kate answered; and the two wives were silent.

Kate was the first to break the silence.

"I am so glad you came to me, Beryl. I

wanted so much to know you. Forgive me for injuring you, though it was unknowingly."

"I do not see what I have to forgive *you*, Kate. It was Dr. Cartland who brought about this sin and trouble."

"Spare me, Beryl—spare me," cried the woman in an agony; "I cannot hear a word against him—of course I know. I know he deserves all that you could say against him; but remember, I not only loved him but I believed in him; and you will know the pain it is to me."

"Poor girl!" answered Beryl, softly, patting the thin hand which she held in hers, "I do understand. I can feel for you. If George were bad, I should love him, and it would be agony to be reminded of it."

"You forgive me, Beryl?"

"Yes."

"Will you ask George to forgive me, too?"

"I do not know where he is, Kate;" and tears trembled on her long lashes.

"He will soon come to you, now," said Kate. "Ask him to forgive me when I am gone," she added, faintly.

Miss Ansell returned that night with a disappointed air.

She had failed to find George Grafton; he was away from town on business.

She had left a letter at his chambers for him; but he might, she felt, return too late, too late to forgive Kate.

In the meantime Beryl remained with Kate, brightening her last hours with her love and kindness; bathing the fevered brow; smoothing the bright, dark hair with gentle hand; cheering the drooping spirit; wiping the death damps from her brow.

A deep affection sprang up between these two young women.

Kate often suffered acutely, and Beryl ministered to her lovingly.

The Lord's day had come round again.

Still Kate was lingering; the church bells were chiming their invite to the Christian to come and hear of Christ. The bells had rung their changes one by one, and now the last gave forth its note—four bells with a warning sound—one, two, three, four! one, two, three, four! ding, dong, ding, dong. You'll be too late; you'll be too late; you'll be too late.

"Do the bells seem to talk to *you*, Beryl? they do to me," said Kate's faint and altered voice. "It is very hard to breathe to-day. You'll be too late; you'll be too late. I wish the bells would say something else, Beryl. Can't you find me fresh words to that old tune, dear?"

"Yes," said Beryl, " many words, Kate—Christ loved the world, Christ loved the world, will go to it."

Kate was lying on her couch by the window, in a loose white wrapper, with still a crimson flower at her breast, pinned there by Beryl (for Kate the dying, loved flowers yet), and Beryl was perched beside her, pillowing the dark head upon her breast, her shining hair mingling with Kate's raven locks, and the two were a perfect picture to look at.

So thought an unseen observer, who finding the door ajar had peeped in, and now stood with a wildly beating heart waiting, trying to regain calmness before he entered the room.

George Grafton—for it was he—never forgot that sight! *His two wives!* the two women whom he had loved, ay, and still loved so fondly, clasped in each others' arms.

I suppose it never occurred to any man before to fall upon such a picture under the like circumstances. It was agony and pleasure combined, and his feelings were impossible to describe.

As he advanced into the room they both looked up, both uttered a faint cry, but it was Kate who spoke.

George gazed at the two beautiful faces —both so perfect in their own style—the faces he had loved so well.

"George, forgive me!" and Beryl made way for him, and kept to the other side of Kate's armless couch.

George knelt down beside his dying wife.

Yes! of the two, *she* was his legal wife; her eyes were fixed eagerly on his, awaiting his reply, while hot tears ran races down Beryl's fair cheeks.

George took her hands in his; he did not find it very easy to speak, but words came at last.

"Kate, my wife, I forgive you as I hope to be forgiven!"

She smiled.

"And now a harder test still, George—can you forgive *him*?"

A pause.

"I forgive him, Kate!"—then silence, broken by Beryl's sobs.

"George," went on the dying woman, "hold me up, I want to speak!" and he supported her with his left arm, while with his right he clasped her clay cold hand.

She smiled, a contented, happy smile.

"I am glad to rest here once more,

George. Beryl has been so good to me, you will repay her dear."

No reply.

"George, don't wait one day after I am put underground. I charge you not to let any delicacy of feeling for me, prevent your atoning for the suffering she has met with through me. Be good to her, George. She is an angel; may God bless you and your little Beryl! I love her as dearly as if she were my sister! *Promise*, George."

"I promise, dear" (with a choking sob).

Kate smiled gloriously.

"Will you kiss me?"

He stooped over her.

"George," she whispered, "I know now that it is too late, I love you—*you* and not another."

Their lips met fondly for the last time.

It was the first and last kiss of *love* Kate had ever given her husband.

Weeping Beryl clung to and kissed the dying hand.

Kate looked from one to the other, and placed Beryl's little hand in George's.

" The bells were wrong, fairy! it was not too late. I am so happy. God bless you both !"

So Kate passed away, and left them hand in hand. She had been the only barrier between them.

She was dead!

CHAPTER XIII.

CONCLUSION.

GEORGE GRAFTON kept his promise, and the day after Kate was laid to rest, he took Beryl home to himself, having legally made her his wife. Very few people ever knew of the Mystery which had so overshadowed his life, threatening to engulf it in blackest ruin and misery, and those few loved George and kept his secret. So no finger was pointed at George and his wife as a "couple with a history." They were very happy these two, with the happiness of perfect love, respect, and confidence. How different would it have been for George, if, looking in Beryl's childish face, he had had to reproach himself with having tarnished her innocence, but he had no such thing to blame himself for, and he was utterly and completely happy, contented, and thankful.

Beryl no longer shunned Kate's name, and she was often talked about by them with hushed voice, as one talks of the beloved dead. There was no sanctum in George's heart *now* where Beryl was shut out, for she too had loved Kate, and thus could think of her while they sat, hand locked in hand, and hearts beating in true response.

George did not go back to Ceylon, nor to business. He and Beryl both loved country life; and they shared it together, living in the lovely county of Monmouth, so dear with historical recollections, beautiful with its wealth of soft sweet scenery and distant blue Welsh mountains, and silvery winding rivers. Not far from the revered old walls of Tintern Abbey, not far from the Wynd Cliff with its dreamy view of vapoury distance, taking in so many counties, where the river winds so brightly among the dark foliage of the trees. Not far from all these lovely gifts of God's own making lived Beryl and George.

Baby George, was baby George no longer; but a sturdy little three-year-old, and that rosy small bundle of white garments sitting on the lawn at Beryl's feet, is little Kate, aged six months. It had been Beryl's proposition to name her so, and George had kissed his wife, and thanked her for her kind thought; so the baby was christened Kate.

What more can be said about them? Except that they were as good as they were happy. No one in trouble, suffering, or sin, ever sought their aid in vain. Would that there were more like them! Surely all must leave them with regret!

Sydney Saunders is too good a fellow to be left out in the cold. He and George were friends, fast friends, and of course he went down to "Silverbeach," where George and Beryl had built their nest; and the time being February, and all the feathered tribe "pairing," Sydney felt bound to follow in the fashion; and Laura Grafton being by his side, why! of course, he proposed to her.

Poor Charles Summers never loved again; but as long as he lives little Beryl will reign in his honest heart.

Kate is done with, the last page of her history closed; still, one line must be written as an epitaph to her memory. With all her faults, she was a queen among women. May God rest her soul!

The elder Graftons are still at Worham, sailing down life's stream together, with some of their children yet around them.

Miss Ansell, you may be sure, is Miss Ansell still, and is likely to remain so; and no one has ever yet found out an instance of her having neglected her duty in any way. She will be a hard old woman to the end; but George's wife, and George's children, can gain smiles from her flinty lips. Yes! and she often smiles to herself with satisfaction, as she remembers that Dr. Cartland never took her in. All along she had felt that he was a villain; all along she had been certain that there was *a Mystery*.

THE END.

www.ingramcontent.com/pod-product-compliance
Lightning Source LLC
Chambersburg PA
CBHW021013240426
43669CB00037B/876